Historic Preservation in Small Towns

A Manual of Practice

Arthur P. Ziegler, Jr.
Walter C. Kidney

American Association for State and Local History
Nashville

Authors and publisher make grateful acknowledgment to the following, for permission to use in this book the photographs credited to them: the National Register of Historic Places; the National Trust for Historic Preservation; Galveston (Tex.) Historical Foundation; Anderson Notter Associates, Inc.; Richard S. Lovelace, Jr.; the Dahlstrom Collection; Galesburg (Ill.) Public Library; Alaska Division of Parks; Fairfield (Conn.) Historic District Commission; Gene Bunnell; Historic American Buildings Survey; Historic Savannah (Ga.) Foundation; Library of Congress; Mary Means; Oregon Historical Society; Preservation/Urban Design, Inc.; William W. Owens, Jr.

Library of Congress Cataloguing-in-Publication Data

Ziegler, Arthur P
  Historic preservation in small towns.

  Bibliography: p.
  Includes index.
   1. Historic buildings — United States — Conservation and restoration. 2. City planning — United States.
  I. Kidney, Walter C., joint author. II. Title.
  E159.Z513   363   79-19422
  ISBN 0-910050-43-0

Publication of this book was made possible in part by funds from the sale of the Bicentennial State Histories, which were supported by the National Endowment for the Humanities.

For
Mary Lib and Delvin Miller,
Rita and Albert Miller,
friends of rural America

Contents

Preface

The major focus of the preservation movement, except for some special historical structures associated with persons important to the development of our nation, has been in our cities. Williamsburg, Virginia, New Harmony, Indiana, and a few others have been the subjects of preservation efforts, too, of course—but of an extraordinary kind, generally executed with funding from outside the towns themselves. The aging urban neighborhood, the Victorian commercial district, the large industrial building, have commanded much of our attention and resources thus far, as well they should. In the past thirty years—and, more notably, in the recent decade—we have developed preservation programs and historic districts in almost every city in the United States, resulting in sophisticated techniques, a body of legislation, and monetary investments not envisioned when restoration work first began at Mount Vernon or even Williamsburg.

Alongside their affection for the city, however, Americans retain an irrepressible wistfulness for the small town, the village, the rural life. The weathered, sun-struck country building, the white clapboard farmhouse nestled under pine trees amidst rolling meadows, or standing frostily in snow, tugs at an American heartstring. The little village around a common green punctuated by church steeples creates an instant sense of harmony within the American soul. Although many Americans prefer the city to live in, the country and the village still symbolize a purity of life, a simplicity of taste, and a candor in human relationships that are so ingrained that any evidence to the contrary goes unnoticed.

Idealization of the country has infused the American character almost from the beginning of our history. Thomas Jefferson (who could at times be more reasoned about city life than many of our leaders) referred to cities as "cesspools." Nathaniel Hawthorne believed it would be useful if cities were periodically burned to the ground. "All towns," he said, in *The Marble Faun,* "should be made capable of purification by fire, or of decay, within each half century."

In light of this national urban enmity, our zest for preserving and restoring the city seems ironic. The chief motivation for it originally came from urban renewal, which suddenly whisked so many of the most familiar older sections of our cities away from us. In fact, one of the few good results of urban renewal as practiced in the 1950s and '60s is the fact that preservationists were stirred to create a countermovement that has resulted in the restoration of thousands of buildings and hundreds of districts. But we had to act fast; the cities got our first attention because there the enemy forces were at work; there the battle raged that ended in a preservation mood growing across America.

Now that we can develop our preservation programs at a more measured pace and based upon a growing experience, we can act with greater choice; not all is crisis. One such option is to try to preserve some of those rural and small-town buildings that have such profound symbolic values for us.

In spite of all of our preservation know-how, this task is difficult for two major reasons.

The first is money. In the cities, we have learned to summon relatively large sums of capital through memberships, community giving campaigns, foundation grants, fund-raising events, and manipulation of federal programs that apply specifically to urban areas. Few such resources exist for the small town.

The second reason is involved with the differences in approach to property in cities and in rural areas. Preservation deals in property; in cities, preservationists buy it and sell it, often with covenants that protect at least the exterior. They seek historic zoning, they demand enforcement of the protective clauses of the Historic Preservation Act of 1966, as well as that all-inclusive protection of buildings from federally financed programs that is expressed in Executive Order 11593. They extend, in effect, the basic concept embodied in all zoning and all environmental protection laws, namely that the right to private property is circumscribed by the public good. Such a view is less prevalent in rural America, where the right to private property is less restricted. Adequate funding and the sophistication of urban give and take are most often lacking in our small towns and rural areas, and architectural preservation, which seems such a necessary and inevitable course of action, is not, for them, so matter-of-course.

All across America, in our urban centers, across our meadows and mountains, too often we see picture windows punched into old houses, aluminum siding added, handsome porches removed, buildings ruined with fads and modernizing, or simply abandoned and left derelict. Fewer voices cry against these ravages in our rural areas, simply because, in our rural areas, there are proportionately fewer people.

Preservation, we repeat, has now reached the point where more time exists for planning, where priorities can be established ahead of time, in an orderly manner, rather than hastily to oppose unexpected onslaughts of insensitive planning. One emerging priority is the preservation of the architecture of rural America.

This manual is meant to offer some techniques that might be considered by those involved in preservation outside the urban parameter. Since our experience is still limited, the book is slim, though it is specific. Generalizations and directives, no matter how apt or hallowed, are not useful to those facing real problems that must be solved. The question is not so much what *should* work as what *has* worked. And can one apply that in some form to the situation one confronts?

Therefore, this is not a planning textbook or a formulation of theories about small-town preservation; it is more nearly a how-to sourcebook— or, rather, a how-some-have-done-it sourcebook. Mr. Kidney and I have included a discussion of some techniques and have then described and asked others to describe successes and failures in a series of specific instances selected for range of approach as well as variety of location. We may not assume that what works in New England will work in New Mexico; therefore, there is geographic as well as technological divergence.

Nearly ten years ago, I wrote a similar manual, called *Historic Preservation in Inner City Areas,* concerning preservation in urban areas, in which I tried to show how we might preserve decaying neighborhoods without massive dislocation of residents. The book struck a sympathetic chord with far more people than I had anticipated and seemed to help many preservation groups in the same spirit. Gary Gore of the American Association for State and Local History encouraged me to work on a similar book for small towns, but a busy schedule prevented concentrated effort. Fortunately, Walter Kidney, with whom I have collaborated in the past, rescued me and provided the bulk of the actual writing. Therefore, we are able to offer this book, which we hope will be of service to those working to preserve the best in the beloved small towns and country places of America.

Arthur P. Ziegler, Jr.

Historic Preservation in Small Towns

1

Introduction: The Nature of the Problem

In this book, a small town will be considered one with up to about 50,000 people. At the same time, we are attempting here to be useful to genuine rural districts, places with isolated farms and occasional cross-road villages. Preservationists who use this book should not, then, apply its techniques without considering their own situation and what is appropriate to it. A town of 50,000 people is a miniature city, impersonal in its ways of conducting public business and with a number of very different, but interested, groups to win over (or prevail against) if anything is to be done. A village or a rural area, on the other hand, is more personal; people know of each other, even if they are not acquainted. In a town, preservationists must organize more formally and proceed in a more formal manner in dealing with local government and with their fellow citizens. In villages and rural districts they must organize, too—must give themselves a name, officers, and bylaws, mainly in order to deal as a unit with outside agencies such as county authorities, state historical commissions, the National Trust, and philanthropic foundations, all of whose help is important.

We are attempting in this book to present a basic toolchest for all such preservationists: to suggest techniques that have worked in other cases, to summarize the current state of the law and present-day funding possibilities, and to tell in some detail what a few American small towns have accomplished.

In a community of any size, a preservationist must justify his ideas. After all, he is presuming to tell people what to do with their property. He is saying to the developer, Do not put up that high-rise; to the storekeeper, Uncover that cast-iron front; to the expanding college or hospital, Do not destroy that block of houses. He is opposing the new to

1

preserve the old, often the old and shabby. He coolly demands expensive repairs and maintenance for ornate buildings and seems to ignore the highest and best use of the land they stand on, with the profit that it promises and the taxes that it imposes. Unless a community is used to the idea of historic preservation, it may well rebel against something so opposed to the routine trends of the real-estate market and ordinary ideas of progress.

The preservationist, however, can argue as follows: most people enjoy beauty and order in their communities. America is full of people who, on vacation, flee the places where they live to see places where other people live. Some want the color and the grandeur of London or Paris, but many are happy in Beacon Hill, Charleston, or Williamsburg, where a simple, quiet dignity prevails. Tourists to these places think that they enjoy the "quaintness," but a part of the pleasure, surely, is in a scene where everything is harmonious in appearance, free of discord and ugliness.

Though this row of Victorian cottages is in Montgomery, Alabama, it might easily stand in any small town in the Deep South. Any single one of these cottages might not be worth a major preservation effort, but together they harmonize—in setback from the street, materials, roof-lines, and other important respects—and they are well worth preserving as a group. —National Register of Historic Places

Those of us involved in preservation realize that, through historic preservation and through thoughtfully planned controls on new development, we might be able to have the same harmony in our own communities.

Also, it is true that most old buildings look good if they are properly repaired and maintained. The builders intended to create something that would be regarded as handsome, after all, by the standards of 1800 or 1870 or 1915, and our own standards are not totally different. If dirty, scabby paint is replaced by fresh paint, if brickwork is washed, if missing cornice brackets are replaced, an old building regains its self-respect and the public rediscovers it. In Pittsburgh, recently, a bar-and-restaurant building of 1900 was restored, mainly by getting rid of the varied remodelings of seven decades and exposing what was underneath; it is a very handsome and popular place these days—and such results are far from unique.

Preservationists know, too, that reusing old buildings, even in new

This might be a grange in almost any part of the rural United States. In fact, it is a former federal courthouse in the Eagle Historic District of Alaska. — Alaska Division of Parks

ways, is often good economics. Often, the shell of a building is likely to be sound, though the wiring and plumbing may need replacement. If that proves true and if the existing building can readily be made to meet the requirements of new users and of the building authorities, there may be no need at all to replace it. Industrial buildings are especially good candidates for adaptive use because of their heavy construction, ample windows, and open floor plans. And old houses have long been used for restaurants, apartments, or offices when they proved too large for any single modern family.

And both preservationists and city promoters know that outsiders, whether they come as tourists or as potential residents, will be attracted to a community that seems to respect itself and to have character and individuality. Decay and haphazard development repel people, unless they have become accustomed to such things over a long period of time.

A small but proud house in Silverton, Colorado. Many small towns have such houses, whose good qualities often go unappreciated until it is too late to preserve them. They reflect the ideas of elegance held in 1870 or 1880—the kinds of things that, in architecture, people are learning to appreciate once more. —Library of Congress. Photograph by Russell Lee

Tourists spend money with local merchants, and new residents spend even more. Local industry and business, if they recruit from outside the region, benefit, too, if it can be shown that the community is a good place to live. Historic preservation helps bring out the soul of the community; it shows that the community has pride and self-awareness.

Houses, business buildings, and churches are not the only objects worthy of preservation. This architecturally treated windmill near Fairfield, Connecticut, is handsome, in itself, and its height makes it literally a landmark. — Fairfield (Connecticut) Historic District Commission

Thus far, historic preservation has been largely a city affair. There are a number of reasons for that—none decisive, but each contributing something. Cities offer a greater number of museums, concerts, and commercial art galleries to enjoy—and to become accustomed to, to want to keep. City dwellers pass through built-up streets and may observe many varied styles of architecture: large, pompous buildings of business and civic centers, restful and often beautiful block fronts of residential neighborhoods. In some fortunate cities, such architectural richness has been accumulating for two centuries or more, giving each neighborhood its peculiar character and making the city as a whole unique.

Works of architecture seldom have any guarantee of immortality, however, as urbanites know all too well. Unless specially protected, a building may come down at any time if the state of the real-estate market urges demolition. A street of mansions becomes slum property or cheap office space, and one by one its houses are stripped, defaced, and at last

A shop, an old school, and two houses on a green in Norwich, Connecticut. The buildings are far from uniform, but there is enough similarity in window size and placement, roof form, and paint color to make them go well together.
—National Register of Historic Places

are demolished entirely for high-rises, stores, warehouses, or parking lots.

Concerned persons, whether they live in metropolitan or rural areas, hate to see that happen, and get together with others, if they can, to prevent it. The urbanite has the advantage of access to more people to form groups to demand for or protest against something. If he loves the architecture of his city, sooner or later he will get together with other people who feel that way, to form a group large enough and loud enough to impress city hall. In places that have elaborate zoning laws and building codes, the preservation groups may attempt to introduce historic-district zoning and try to get the building code modified in a way that allows old buildings to go on functioning, perhaps for new purposes. Such groups will inform themselves about the help that funding agencies may give—say, in providing money for a revolving fund—and the expert advice available from the National Trust. The group may well have in its

A row of houses in the Fernandina Beach Historic District, Florida. The two closest houses are to the same design, but all four go well together. — National Register of Historic Places. Photograph by Karl Holland

membership an architect or two who will volunteer advice to property owners.

More easily than his rural counterpart, the city dweller is often able to reach government agencies and philanthropic foundations that may provide help. Furthermore, he is often trying to save something very well known—a work of American architecture, perhaps, illustrated in every history book, or twenty blocks of houses known to every tourist. Whether he succeeds or fails, he is almost bound to find a good deal of sympathy for his proposals.

The small-town or rural preservationist has had fewer advantages. Many small communities, for instance, do not have a zoning law. Their inhabitants are used to few restrictions on use of property within the

A small town often has its showplaces, the homes of wealthy families. What is to be done when no single family is willing or able to occupy all of such a house? Some are torn down, and the town loses a part of its older character and charm, while the buildings that replace those removed are all too often ugly. At other times, aging mansions become offices, apartments, or mixtures of both. Ideally, preservationists try to match buildings that should be saved with current demand for space that families and businesses need. The house shown here, the Mercer-Wilder house in Savannah, Georgia, was saved from demolition by preservationists. — Historic Savannah Foundation. Photograph by Leopold Adler II

community. Often, fewer people in small communities step forward to assume responsibility for conserving the area's notable architecture or aspects of the landscape—things valuable because they *look* the way they do; thus it is often harder for a small town or rural community to form

Every community has its individualists, who see and do things their own way. Sometimes their individualism finds an outlet in houses, such as this one from Thomasville, Georgia, of about 1885. — National Register of Historic places. Photograph by David J. Kaminsky

an effective civic group. Political conditions are likely to be different, too; governmental regulations may stem mainly from a remote county seat or from the state capital and seem less immediate and less controllable than in the city. Massive development seems less likely, especially in a rural area, unless the area is obviously being suburbanized. The defenses seem hardly worth maintaining until outrageous development begins; then it is, to some extent, too late. There must be many citizens of small communities who, by temperament, are preservationists but who, for various reasons, have never become militant in the cause of preservation.

Now, however, things are beginning to change. Against all predictions, city dwellers are moving *back* to the sort of small town their parents or grandparents may have left. Some industries have moved away from the city and taken many of their workers with them. The small town, even more than the suburb, seems to many to offer the basic good things of life, and many of the young, so far as possible, are trying to move even

Depending on what part of the United States you are in, the nature of a historic district is likely to differ. This is Silver City, Idaho, a mining town: architecturally plain, but a reminder of the state's past. — National Register of Historic Places. Photograph by Idaho State Historical Society

farther out, into the midst of nature. Some of these former urbanites are not at all interested in their surroundings, but some are the same sorts of people who have been the force behind historic preservation in the city. Such people are likely to be helpful to the leaders of small communities in spreading the preservationist gospel across the country.

The average preservationist in a small town and his average neighbor may not see eye to eye. Whether the community has conventional zoning or not, the idea of historic-district zoning may well seem, to some, unnecessary. So may alternative conceptions, such as facade and scenic easements. Furthermore, small-town neighbors may clash over matters of taste in preservation. The average small town has experienced hopeful spasms of modernization from time to time, especially along Main Street. It may have a double row of ornate electric lamp posts from 1910 and an occasional patch of Carrara glass on a shopfront from the "Modernize

A street in Galena, Illinois, in 1969. Here is a typical small-town commercial street. On the one hand, the buildings, though simple and undistinguished, go well together and could be the architectural background of a very pleasant street. On the other hand, the signs, of all sizes and shapes, bearing varied forms of lettering, confuse the look of the street, while the closely parked cars give it a cluttered appearance and reduce the space open to moving traffic. A harmonious scheme for signs and the provision of convenient back-of-store parking would be a great help. — National Trust for Historic Preservation. Photograph by Bruce Krimskey

Main Street'' campaigns of the 1930s. In more recent decades, salesmen of ready-made facings have probably passed through again and again. The outlying shopping centers have goaded the town's merchants into emulation, and the local branches of the food chain, the gas-and-oil chain, and the motel chain have suggested new architectural mannerisms to the merchants and bar owners. This is the way it is on Main Street, and the same may be so elsewhere in town. The old courthouse may already have been replaced by something more or less in the manner of Edward Stone, a box decorated with false, outsized arcading.

Now comes the preservationist, assuring everyone that the much-covered cast iron of 1870, the chipped stonework of 1900, were really the best things on Main Street, after all, and that the old courthouse—if it has survived—is a handsome building, full of character. Such revelations may be a little hard to take. The preservationist will have to show that the old facades, properly treated, will come up with a smile and that customers, house buyers, lending agencies, and others are capable of smiling back. Nor is it enough to preserve, even to restore, a building here and there, unless the idea of preservation spreads. One proud Victorian front will not divert many customers back to Main Street, and a set of handsomely restored rooms will not compensate fully for squalor outside every window.

In a way, a preservationist is an arranger of truces. He coaxes everyone on a street to do what is best for all, in pleasure and profit, even if each person has to sacrifice some of his personal inclinations in the process. On Main Street, the preservationist may try to strip off the cheap modern veneers and get the raucous signs down. If he succeeds, Main Street looks more attractive than before; similarly, a street of houses is pleasanter to live in if it is not broken up by gas stations, fast-food outlets, and other disruptive places. But the preservationist has to show that he has something to offer that more than substitutes for the convenience of having these things just down the street. He also has to accept the fact that, in our modern world, these things will have to go *somewhere;* a demand for them exists, and it will be met. The preservationist, if he is realistic, will think in terms of a whole modern community in which change is accepted, though controlled. The old is to be appreciated for its beauty and its continuing usefulness, and to be made whole and fresh; the new is to fit gracefully into the existing town or its environs.

2
Some Considerations and Techniques

The Nature of Your Intentions

Begin by being honest with yourself. What do you want to see done? If you are reading this book, you probably wish to see some of the architecture or landscape of your community saved from damaging alterations, possibly even restored to its appearance when new and fresh. Others in the community may agree with you, but you will have to find and organize them. Many more will disagree with you, because you will be telling them what to do with their property.

It is important, then, to know what you are aiming for, and why. Do you admire the old architecture of your community and feel that new construction cannot be as beautiful? Do you feel that it will save money to rehabilitate old buildings instead of tearing them down and starting from scratch? Are you thinking about attracting tourists? Do you love your town's history, or your region's history, and wish to preserve the things that remind you of it? Know exactly what it is you are after, why you are doing what you are doing. Knowing these things will help in your planning and in your work of persuading others.

These days, people are very suspicious of "elitism," the tendency to shape the world to suit a small, powerful group of people. A preservationist should face the question of whether what he is doing is or is not elitist. He is certainly imposing his personal taste on others—and at their expense—every time he demands that they retain clapboard and keep it painted rather than covering it with aluminum or vinyl siding that stays white without being painted. Perhaps the preservationist should admit that he *is* elitist, but promise that, when people see how beautiful their preserved community is, they too will join the elite.

Forming an Organization

Preservation groups are usually formed, almost spontaneously, when some outrage to the local landscape has been the last straw. By then, of

13

course, it is too late to undo a major piece of damage. The best time to form a preservation group is *before* any great harm has been done. It is fairer to persons who wish to alter their property, too, if they know that an organization exists whose policies are on record as disapproving of certain changes besides those forbidden by zoning ordinances and the building codes.

Begin by looking around your community and trying to see what is beautiful and interesting about it in its present state. Take no feature of a landscape or of a street for granted; if it is physical, it can be changed. Talk with others who seem to enjoy these things, and sound them on their willingness to combine in a small group. If there is a local historical society, its members may be the ones to approach first.

Start off modestly, but with some formality: select a name for the organization, draw up by-laws, elect officers, plan a budget for publications. The formality may seem a little ridiculous at first, but some day you will want help (perhaps including money) from local, state, or federal authorities, and at that time you will have to be functioning as a bona fide

Old industrial buildings, like the Old Stone Mill in Decorah, Iowa, pictured here, help to reveal the history of a region. Such structures can often be adapted for use as stores or offices and may sometimes continue to be used industrially.—National Register of Historic Places. Photograph by Darrell D. Henning

Lighthouses, such as this one at Cape Elizabeth, Maine, are distinctive features of many coastal ports. As electronic ship-to-shore navigational equipment grows more sophisticated, it sometimes happens that lighthouses at some locations may no longer be needed for their original purposes. Should the Coast Guard phase out such a specialized structure, local preservationists should make every attempt to preserve it. With ingenuity, adaptive uses can often be made of the building's varied components. — National Register of Historic Places

organization. If your organization is a mature, long-active one, you are more likely to receive favorable attention.

Your first organization may be a group of private citizens, with no more political influence than any other citizens' group has; but look forward to the day when your community (if the laws of your state allow it) can be persuaded to establish a historical district commission. Such a commission has legal powers to halt or delay reconstruction or demolition inside a historic district (see below), and is thus a very important tool for historic or scenic preservation.

A useful guide to organization-forming is Michael J. Smith's, *Heritage Projects: A Practical Guide for Community Preservation Organizations,* published by the Michigan Department of State in 1975. (The bibliography at the end of this book should be consulted for reading material useful to supplement information given here.)

Surveys

As soon as you can, have a survey made of what you are trying to save, property by property. This serves two purposes. First, it gets all the important information about any given property in one place. Second, it gives you moral support in any appeal to preserve or restore a property. We will take these two matters in detail.

Let us assume, on the matter of important information, that the property contains a house. The survey form, a piece of paper for that property, will begin with the name by which the house is known, often the name of the original owner, the present owner, or both. Then it will give the address. Somewhere the date of construction will appear, and the name of its architect (or, if there was no architect, its builder). There will be information on any major reconstructions, with their dates. In a few words, the form will describe the architectural style, call attention to interesting features of the house, and say something about the families that have lived there and about any importance in history the building may have. Usually, there will be one or more photographs of the house. Some survey forms will call for other information, but the types given above are standard.

A great many kinds of survey forms are now in use. The National Trust for Historic Preservation (see Appendix 1) has forms that can be used, but some preservation groups have made up their own. If possible, a professional consultant or your state historic preservation officer should take charge of the survey; not only can he do research necessary to obtain some of the historical facts, but he knows the type of information useful for entering on the forms. Volunteers trained by the consultant can conduct the house-to-house canvass under his direction.

Let us return for a moment to the state historic preservation officer (sometimes called the SHPO). He is a very good man to get acquainted with early in your efforts, in part because of his connections with federal agencies. In fact, it will be very hard to avoid getting to know him, since he is responsible for doing a comprehensive survey of the places in your state that are nationally or locally important for historical or cultural reasons. The survey forms he uses are probably the best to use, and because of his obligation to create his comprehensive survey by 1983, your own survey can probably be done by him at times free of any charge

In the East and the South are many communities with an eighteenth- or early nineteenth-century flavor, such as appears in this distinguished small-town street in Frederick, Maryland. The business buildings shown here date mostly from the late nineteenth and early twentieth centuries and are larger than the original buildings on their sites. Keeping such buildings is much better than trying to reproduce the Colonial style in a new building constructed with present-day methods to meet present-day demands. — National Register of Historic Places

to you; at other times, the SHPO may offer you matching funds so that you can carry out the survey on your own.

The survey can have a great moral effect on the community. Many people not really interested in architecture or landscape will be surprised, even flattered, to find their properties praised in a survey. This encourages them to take new pride in their properties and to think twice about any change that the survey indicates would remove the properties' good features. If the survey is published (see below), its effect on property owners will be all the greater; people are naturally proud to see their homes, the churches they belong to, or any places connected with them praised publicly. The survey attests that old buildings, probably long taken for granted, are to be taken seriously.

Two kinds of survey are possible: those that show every property, interesting or not, in the area covered, and those that show only the properties worth preserving or restoring. The second kind is easier to prepare, since there are fewer forms to fill out; but in cases where a property should have been included, but was not, a special research and photographing job is necessary to remedy the error.

Survey work can be expensive, even with volunteers and especially if you hire a private consultant. Fortunately, some federal money is available to help. Your state historic preservation officer, through his connections with the National Register of Historic Places (see below), has access to money to help make surveys intended to find properties to put on the Register. The National Trust for Historic Preservation has a consultant grant service program intended to pay consultant fees. And money can sometimes come through the Architectural and Environmental Arts Program of the National Endowment for the Arts.

The National Registers

The National Historic Preservation Act of 1966 authorizes the Secretary of the Interior to maintain a National Register of Historic Landmarks and a National Register of Historic Places. The Historic Landmarks register is a list of about a thousand places regarded as of outstanding importance in American history. The Historic Places register has many more listings, and when preservationists talk of the "National Register," this is the one they usually mean.

There are several good reasons for trying to get the most important properties in your community onto the National Register. First, acceptance of a property for listing in the Register is evidence that the federal government—specifically, the Heritage, Conservation, and Recreation

Service of the National Park Service—regards the property as important to save.

Second, National Register listing makes it very difficult for the federal government to injure, or even help in injuring, a property. Under Section 106 of the National Historic Preservation Act of 1966, the President's Advisory Council on Historic Preservation must be given the opportunity to comment on any proposed action affecting a National Register property that would be (1) done by a federal agency; (2) licensed by a federal agency; or (3) done with the federal financial help (unless Revenue-Sharing money is used). Any federal agency whose actions

A street corner in Frederick, Maryland, showing a public building of the mid-nineteenth century and what appears to be a Colonial house with late nineteenth-century alterations in an imitation Colonial style. In a very old town, such Victorian architecture is often ignored, torn down, or cheaply made over to look Colonial; and yet, the Victorian buildings often are—as we are beginning to realize—good, in their own way, and preserving them should become one of our top priorities.—National Register of Historic Places. Photograph by Ted Lowe

might lead to the injury of a National Register property can be forced to justify and take responsibility for what it is doing. Furthermore, Executive Order 11593 of 1971 directs federal agencies to take no action that might lead to injury to a National Register property without consulting the Advisory Council.

Third, the National Park Service offers money to assist local groups in surveys, planning, acquisition, and development connected with National Register properties. This money, channeled through the state historic preservation officer, can amount to 50 percent of the total cost. The balance is to be money from the state, local government, or private sources and/or services, property, and materials donated for the project.

Fourth, there are federal tax benefits for the preservation and restoration of National Register income-producing properties by owners or

The John Whipple house, dating from the mid-seventeenth century, in Ipswich, Massachusetts. The house has been restored to its original appearance. Historic preservation started out in this country more than a hundred years ago, saving places such as this one, reminders of the nation's early past. Yet, even so recently as fifteen years ago, houses not much newer than the Whipple House were in danger of demolition in Ipswich. —William W. Owens, Jr.

long-term (over thirty years) lessees. On the one hand, restoration costs may be amortized over a five-year period for tax purposes; on the other, demolition of such a property is no longer tax-deductible.

Fifth, residential buildings on the National Register or regarded as eligible for the National Register are eligible for FHA Historic Preservation Loans from local, FHA-insured banks, under the Title 1 Home Improvement Loan Program of the National Housing Act. (Incidentally, *any* home in an officially designated historic district is eligible for such a loan).

Criteria for National Register listing are basically these. *Eligible:* Places associated with great events; places associated with great persons; places interesting architecturally; places interesting to historians in any way. *Ordinarily not eligible:* Cemeteries and tombs; places in active use by religious groups; historic buildings that have been moved; copies of historic buildings; buildings that otherwise might be eligible but that became significant less than fifty years ago.

Your state historic preservation officer keeps a list of National Register properties in your state. He can also send you the forms needed to apply for National Register status on behalf of an unlisted property.

Obtaining National Register listing is a slow and complicated process. The form requires the applicant to state names by which the property in question is known; list the address of the property; state what type of property it is—building, district, etc.; specify ownership (public or private); say whether it is, or may become, publicly owned; note whether it is occupied or deserted; state whether the public has access to it; explain how it is used; give name and address of owner; state where the legal description of the property is filed; show what existing surveys include it; explain why it is significant (space for an essay is included); specify its present condition and appearance (space for another essay, including any known information on its appearance in the past); cite books, etc., in which it is mentioned; give precise location according to official map reference standards; specify size of the property; and provide the name of the person preparing the form. Photographs and a map showing the location of the property must be included. If a historic district is involved, rather than a single property, descriptions and photographs of all properties in the district will be needed.

The National Register form is filled out by local preservationists, then sent to the state historic preservation officer for approval. If he approves it, the property is listed on the State Register of Historic Places and, if you request it, the form is passed on to the National Park Service in Washington for consideration on the National Register. Nonapproval by the SHPO does not necessarily keep the property in question from

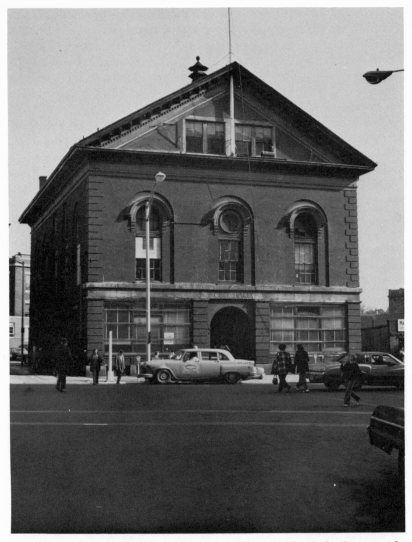

One obvious type of building to save is an old town hall, which often provides space for public meetings as well as space for offices or shops. This example, from the middle of the nineteenth century, is in Malden, Massachusetts. — Photograph by Gene Bunnell

National Register listing, since you can appeal his decision to the Keeper of the National Register, but there is no appeal from the Keeper's decision.

The process of getting National Register listing takes from six months to three years.

Publications and Publicity

You will probably want to go into print at some point, though your individual situation will determine exactly what you will publish.

One obvious candidate for publication is your survey. A fairly large town like Biloxi, Mississippi (population about 45,000), produced a 172-page paperbound book in 1976 in which 218 buildings were illustrated, each with at least one photograph and some with plans and drawings. In addition, there were both a general and an architectural history of Biloxi, a glossary defining architectural terms, a list of books giving useful information, and an index. Publication was subsidized by a federal Community Development Grant, and the book sold for five dollars. On the other hand, the Historic District Study Committee of Old Lyme, Connecticut (population 400), incorporated part of its survey in the free *Report* that was important in getting ratification of historic district zoning. Of 71 buildings in the proposed district, 19 were illustrated and described.

It should be noted that a rural region can be written about as readily as a town or a village, though it may not be possible to give every place of interest. *On the Mountain, in the Valley,* published in 1977 by the Catskill Center for Conservation and Development, is a case in point. Covering portions of seven New York counties, this book gives a good general view of Catskill Mountain architecture, is well illustrated, and carries a short history of the region.

All such books help make the public conscious of the landscape and architecture of the places where they live and help raise doubts in the minds of those who might otherwise injure properties, possibly without knowing what they are about.

It is not enough, however, to copy the information on your survey forms as a book manuscript. That makes for a dry book, and often one that both includes unnecessary information and leaves out some data useful to the public. A typical architectural survey, as published, might include a map at the front or the back, showing the places described; an essay on the history of the town or region and its architecture; an account of the historic-preservation group and its aims and accomplishments; the main section of the book, describing and illustrating each building of interest; a glossary, explaining unfamiliar architectural terms; a list of books and articles that might interest the reader who wanted to know more; and, somewhere, an acknowledgments section thanking agencies and persons who helped in writing and publishing the book.

The main section of the book, that on the individual buildings, should have the following information, in more or less this order: (1) name of building; (2) address; (3) date built, with dates of major additions or remodelings; (4) name of person responsible for its design, whether architect or builder; (5) style of architecture; (6) any interesting information about the architectural features and the history of the building; (7) in most cases, a photograph of the building. Sometimes other information from the survey sheets will appear, such as an estimation of the building's architectural or historic importance, or of its present physical condition. In discussing the interesting aspects of the building, try to be brief and to the point. It is hard to decide, sometimes, whether a story about the building's past is interesting in an architectural survey, or even whether it is true. Anecdotes that have nothing much to do with a building's

To work effectively, a preservationist needs full measures of imagination, faith, and determination. Before preservationists began restoration, it was clear, from the flaked paint, boarded-up openings, and general air of disuse and abandonment, that this row of buildings in Newburyport, Massachusetts, was waiting for death. —Anderson Notter Finegold, Inc.

architectural or historic importance should be judged with a severe eye and probably left out. Drawings are sometimes used in place of photographs, but it is rare for them to be as good.

The National Trust has a publication grant program that may help you with money to publish your survey. For this and other sources of financial aid in publishing, consult your state preservation officer, or the National Trust.

In addition to a published survey, you may want to print pamphlets appealing for funds, posters announcing house tours and street fairs, and other occasional items that remind the public of your existence and serve particular purposes. As far as possible, make these neat, interesting, and attractive, so that the public notices them and so that your organization gives the impression of doing everything well. It helps if you have a symbol of some sort, a kind of trademark, that appears on everything you do. People remember such a device.

Signs are important, too. If you are restoring a house or reselling a

Photographed after restoration, these Newburyport, Massachusetts, buildings show what preservationists had the imagination to see and the faith and determination to accomplish. The results may be a bit self-consciously "quaint," but the row of buildings has been brought back to life. Notice the removal of utility poles, the brick paving, and the small, well-executed shop signs. —Phokion Karas, courtesy of Anderson Notter Finegold, Inc.

house for restoration, put up a sign with your name and symbol on it, telling people what you are doing. If there are really old houses in your community, you may want to offer the owners small plaques with the date of construction on them. This is a good practice to follow, since it suggests to both the owners and their neighbors that an old building, rooted in the community's history, is something to be proud of. The plaques can go further, saying something about the history of the building; remember, however, that they have to be kept small, or owners will be shy of putting them up.

In addition, signs at the outskirts of town can identify a historic district and invite visitors to it. Publicizing sites in this way can be a good thing for the businesses of the district, by the way—not only may tourists want to buy things while they are there, but such signs identify the district as a special place to your fellow-citizens, who shop regularly. A sign urging a visit to a museum building is useful, of course, especially if an admission is charged.

In your work of making the community preservation-conscious, you can also get others to publish for you. As a serious, respectable organization, and an active one, you should be able to get local newspapers and television stations interested in your work: not at first, perhaps, but after some drum-beating and a little solid accomplishment. Consider an occasional newspaper article on an architecturally or historically interesting building—perhaps even a series of articles on such buildings. People who read about them are more likely to visit them. Perhaps the local television station could be persuaded to do a documentary on the preservation campaign you are mounting, mentioning, as one aspect, the economic successes of such campaigns in other places like yours. Regional newspapers and radio stations are interested in local affairs, especially when the names of local people are mentioned, and will sometimes use a news release just as it is given to them. Have well-written releases, with pictures for the newspapers, sent out when you have accomplished something or wish to announce a house tour, fund-raising campaign, or anything else that requires public support.

When people become aware of your work and show an interest, you should perhaps invite an architect or planner with experience in historic preservation to lecture. If he has a chance to walk around your community, he may not only be able to talk about his experiences elsewhere but speak, as a well-traveled authority, of the good points of what you are trying to save—even offer suggestions as to what should be done.

Students and professors from local colleges may be able to help, in various ways, in your promotional efforts: designing posters, handing out leaflets, and in various other ways. See if you can get them interested.

Finally, consider events of the holiday type. The historic-building tour is a classic, tried-and-true device both for raising money and inspiring public interest. If you can get a half-dozen or more historic buildings, restored or not restored, to open their doors, you have the makings of a tour. Sell passes, have a person in each building on the tour who can talk about it, print leaflets repeating the information, and serve refreshments somewhere along the way; that is about all there is to it. Not all the buildings need be restored; in fact, it might be useful to include a run-down building that would look fine if an understanding person took it in hand. Someone on your tour might be inspired to do just such a thing, or at least to contribute money toward getting it done. A variation on the building tour is the progressive dinner. Here, people on the tour eat a complete dinner, cooked after recipes of a century or so ago, by going from building to building; a different course is served at each location.

A festival (see below) can not only raise money for you, but will help people see what you are trying to do.

Once a tannery, this abandoned industrial building in Peabody, Massachusetts, was part of the Crowninshield Estates. Seen here before restoration, it is useless, deteriorating, grim—even sinister-looking. —Anderson Notter Finegold, Inc.

Legal Devices

The laws that encourage or permit the devices given below differ from state to state, and you should check with your state historic preservation officer before attempting to use them. Unless you have legal support on either a state or local level, an owner who objects to being bound by such devices can win in a lawsuit.

Property ownership has been called a "bundle of rights." Thus, if you have coal on your land, you can sell the mineral rights to a mining company. You have sold them the coal and, so far as state and federal laws permit, the right to remove it. The bundle of rights is never absolute. Under the power of eminent domain, a government organization can take your land and give you money in return. If you fail to pay taxes or other debts, you may lose the property as well. The theory is that when one or more rights in the bundle called *ownership* are taken from you, it is done in a way that is fair to you.

Historic preservation often works best if it can withdraw and keep a right or two from the bundle. Consider, for instance, the *covenant*. A covenant is a special agreement put into a deed when a property is sold. Through a covenant, the preservation organization can sell the whole bundle of rights to a house, except, for instance, the right to alter the exterior, which it keeps for itself and never exercises. In return, the owner gets a house whose exterior may have been fully restored (Historic Charleston, South Carolina, sells houses that way); or the buyer may get a break on the selling price, or simply the pleasure and advantage of having a building of distinction.

Similar to the covenant is the *easement*. An easement is a transfer of a property right without an actual sale of the property. A rural homeowner who wants a telephone may have to grant the phone company an easement, for instance, to string its line all the way across his property to reach properties beyond. Whatever he does with his property afterwards must not disturb the line. Preservationists can either buy easements from property owners or, if they are lucky, have them given. Once sold or given, easements "run with the land," and are binding on all property owners up to some distant date.

Owners sometimes grant easements free of charge, because they are proud of their homes and want them to remain unaltered even after they move away or die. Often, however, an owner thinks that he owes it to himself to demand at least a token payment. And, as he usually keeps the responsibility, and the wish, to maintain his property in good condition, some money toward doing so is only fair. The preservation organization, as part of its bargain with the owner, should offer professional advice on repairs and maintenance and should help the owner obtain any public money available to help with the upkeep. The organization should also call the owner's attention to any property tax deductions available to an owner who grants an easement.

The commonest sort of easement on property is the *facade easement,* through which the owner agrees not to change any part of the building's exterior—at least, in the parts that the public usually sees. A house owner may agree, for instance, not to change the front and sides without the preservation group's permission, but retain the right to change the rear as he pleases, adding or demolishing to suit his family's needs. But there are also easements on the interior decoration and even on the structure of a building. All that has to be spelled out carefully in the agreements written up.

In some states, notably in Virginia, *scenic easements* are allowed by law and are fairly popular. Instead of simply protecting a building, such easements also protect land. Development of open land is restricted, so

Sturdy, well-lighted, adaptable to many modern purposes, the big brick factory buildings of the nineteenth century have great potential for continued use. The Crowninshield Estates, in Peabody, Massachusetts, once a tannery, is now an attractive apartment complex. —Phokion Karas, courtesy of Anderson Notter Finegold, Inc.

that a farm or an estate retains its rural character. The easement usually covers certain buildings, or at least those sides of buildings that can be seen from a public road. Once again, such easements can be granted free of charge or offered for a fee.

Such easements are encouraged if the state and local governments are sympathetic in their policy of property taxation. Taxation, usually, is based on the "highest and best"—in other words, most profitable—uses permitted by zoning laws or by the state of the local real estate market. If it seems possible to build a lucrative shopping center on the site of a group of homes, the land on which the houses stand may be taxed *as if* there were a shopping center there already. But if an easement protects a home *as* a home, a farm *as* a farm, and if it is legally binding, then "highest and best," according to ordinary zoning laws or the real-estate market, may not apply. In effect, the home gets a special residential zoning; and, when it is sold, the new buyer purchases beauty, antiquity, and the distinction that comes from having such things. Even on the real-estate market, his is a special case.

Historic-district zoning is another matter. Instead of offering rewards by individual agreement with owners, historic district zoning imposes restrictions on owners. Such zoning is in addition to any conventional zoning law that may cover the district, and it has a different purpose. Conventional zoning limits the uses to which a property may be put; historic-district zoning limits the physical alterations that may be made to the property. Under conventional zoning, it might be forbidden to turn a house into a factory; under historic-district zoning, it might be forbidden, or at least made difficult, to reface the house with aluminum siding. Historic district zoning says that no alterations of certain kinds (especially where the public could see them) may be made without going through a special legal process that may take up to a year. Typically, such zoning allows a historical district commission to hold up a demolition or building permit that local government would otherwise issue promptly. The commission can attempt, for a specified period, to reason with the owner, suggest other ways of solving his problem, put public pressure on him. Its authority to stop him outright from a bad change in the property never lasts forever, but it can leave him for a while with property on his hands that he regards as useless in its present form. Speculative builders are especially vulnerable in such a situation; often they operate on a shoestring and have to start making money soon after they invest it. (And in fairness to these builders, among others, it is good to establish a clearly thought-out, clearly stated, unchanging preservation policy in your community as soon as possible.)

The Tax Reform Act of 1976 provides certain federal tax incentives (i.e., "tax breaks") for the preservation and rehabilitation of buildings that are certified, in one way or another, as historic. We will discuss the Act more fully later, but should point out that it applies, among other things, to buildings that are located in a historic district listed on the National Register and that are certified as being historic, or are located in a historic district so certified by the state or local government, if the statute designating the district is also certified (approved) by the U.S. Secretary of the Interior. (An owner may request through the state historic preservation officer, that his building be certified as *not* historic.) The tax incentives (see "Finance," below, for details) reward preservation of historic properties and repairs and remodelings that maintain their character, while penalizing demolitions. The area survey is most useful in administering a historic-zoning policy. You can fight to the death for certain buildings, put up a good fight for others, let others go with mild regret, and welcome the demolition of still others. When you survey the area, simply rate the buildings according to a scale of four or five categories of worth. You are on record—to yourselves and to the public—as to your attitudes toward

A close-up of the restored Crowninshield Estates of Peabody, Massachusetts, shows use of industrial artifacts, such as vats and machinery parts, in landscaping the area when the former tannery was made into an apartment complex.
—Phokion Karas, courtesy of Anderson Notter Finegold, Inc.

them and can go into action without having to rethink the whole matter in every instance. You may surprise yourself and others by suddenly discovering the beauty of a property, but such surprises can be kept to a minimum.

The survey is also useful if property owners fight your historic-district zoning law in court. If the law contains carefully considered and carefully stated criteria for evaluating properties—if it says, as clearly as possible, *why* one property is valuable and another is not—then the courts may support your zoning law. If, on the other hand, your criteria are vague, your zoning law will be overthrown. There are two subtleties to keep in mind, in drafting a historic-zoning law. The first is that any given property—especially a building—may not be very interesting in itself, but it may create a harmonious scene with several other such properties. For instance, a street of plain houses a hundred years old may contain not one authentic gem of architecture, *but*—if two of the houses are torn down for a fast-food chain and its driveways, a restful, satisfying block front may be reduced to a visual mess. Most American houses, if you look

This row of store buildings in Ann Arbor, Michigan, has lost its cornice, which once jutted from the top of the wall, and there is obvious room for improvement in treatment of the individual store fronts; yet, the projecting signs that are so distracting in many such shopping rows are not present here. — Preservation/Urban Design, Inc.

beneath the ornament, are foursquare boxes with sash windows regularly disposed in flat fronts. One house may have colonial ornament from 1770 at its doorway and roof eaves, another have Italian-style ornament from 1860, and another one imitation colonial ornament from 1910, but the basic shapes of such houses are often the same, and in most instances the dimensions of their windows are about the same, too. The actual decoration would be just a part of the total effect, and so the houses would be good architectural neighbors. Sometimes, of course, a house can be different from those alongside it in every respect, yet be so good in its own way that it would be a mistake to give it up. And, as we have said, the ordinary, dull house that harmonizes in its general form with its neighbors may be the best that can be reasonably expected, ordinary modern construction being what it is. Use imagination, then: think of the whole scene as it might be, in deciding what buildings to preserve.

The second subtlety: Think of what may be built in the future in a historic district. Do not ask for exact reproductions of old buildings. And do not treat mere decoration, because you are told it is colonial, as a justification for building something new in a truly colonial neighborhood. Demand buildings that harmonize in shape, building materials, and other visual aspects with the historic buildings around them. Such buildings

Bannack, first territorial capital of Montana: now a ghost town. — National Register of Historic Places. Photograph by George Grant

need not profess to be in any historic style; what counts is that the materials the public sees, the forms of house windows and doorways, the height of walls, be more or less like those of the buildings you have been trying to preserve, that they have compatibility. In cases where a building *must* be different—a church, a store, a civic auditorium, for example, in the midst of old homes—you are in the laps of the gods. Not too many architects know how to fit such large-scale, modern constructions into historic neighborhoods; not too many even care. If an architectural historian has been involved with your project, he may be able to help.

In any event, it might be useful to draw up some architectural design standards, as has been done in Hudson, Ohio (see below), or Savannah, Georgia. Such standards are not infallible, but they form some basis for censorship of new construction in places you are trying to preserve.

The National Endowment for the Arts may be able to help, through financial support, a local program for establishing criteria to be used by those remodeling historic buildings or designing new ones for a historic district. If you are trying to develop such criteria, it is worth getting in touch with the NEA.

Master Planning

Many communities have a plan that determines how their different areas will be used, how traffic will be accommodated, and what kinds of construction will be permitted. Zoning, which governs land use and the maximum size of construction on a given property, is part of such a plan. The purpose of ordinary zoning is to prevent something from being built in a certain part of the community that would spoil things for everyone else there. Some communities, however, have the *historic district zoning* just mentioned. Within a certain closed line on the maps, nothing can be changed, demolished, or (sometimes) built without the permission of a group (called a historical district commission or board of architectural review) whose function is to see that the qualities that make the district historically or architecturally interesting are preserved. Such a group can usually not stave off an unwelcome building or demolition project forever, but they can slow it down so much that property owners or developers are usually willing to reach some sort of compromise. (The permission of the historical district commission, by the way, is in addition to the usual building permit that ensures that the project will be safe and in accordance with the building code for the whole community.) If your state laws encourage the creation of historic district commissions, and if you have many interesting properties in one area, the creation of a historic district is worth thinking of.

Besides trying to establish a historic district, you should try to see that

In many small towns and villages, the churches are the most prominent buildings. Fortunately, they are usually well maintained and usually are safe from demolition; but sometimes a preservationist may need to suggest modernization of an old church in ways that preserve its original appearance, to avoid inappropriate "modernizing" that would destroy the building's integrity or to prevent its being replaced by a completely new structure. If an old church building is no longer needed for religious services, preservationists can often help by suggesting conversion of the building for other uses, rather than having it torn down. The handsome structure shown here is St. Mary's-in-the-Mountains, Virginia City, Nevada. —Historic American Buildings Survey

all new street and road plans, commercial development plans, and other plans for the whole community or the whole region are done in a way that will not injure but, rather, will help your preservation campaign. If your community is having planning done, insist that the planners include persons who care about historic places such as those you are trying to protect. Such places need defenders against the usual sort of town planner, highway engineer, developer, or chamber of commerce promoter, who will not understand what is good about old buildings or "unimproved" land. A planner who understands those things, yet realizes that the community has traffic to move and that it hopes for commercial growth, may be able to develop a scheme for the whole community that will, sooner or later, be accepted by everyone.

Two kinds of plan for your community are possible. The first is a true

New England town halls were often combinations of municipal offices with civic auditoriums. This one, in Littleton, New Hampshire, shows the prominence a town hall can gain through size and elaboration. It also hints at the problems of fire safety and heat conservation to be considered in modernizing such a structure, often built entirely of wood. — National Register of Historic Places. Photograph by Lawrence H. Presby

master plan, examining and prescribing the future development of every part of your community. Historic preservation should be a part of that master plan, but it will include much more besides. The second kind of plan is a *historic preservation plan,* pure and simple, one with little to say about the community as a whole. The first kind of plan is better, though more expensive, of course; it builds historic preservation into the future of the whole community, preventing a good many unpleasant surprises and conflicts. It does include the danger, however, that your interests may not be the only ones considered and that unless the planners are interested in historic preservation—and unless your community officials are interested—historic preservation may not get its fair share of consideration. If a planning organization is going to be employed to devise a master plan for the whole community, you may want to demand that a firm of historic preservation consultants be employed to advise them.

Federal and state money is generally available to help communities obtain master plans. Furthermore, the National Trust for Historic Preservation has a Consultant Service Grant Program that helps pay for historic preservation plans; it also has a list of recommended consultants for making such plans.

Old houses, unrestored, at Plymouth, New Hampshire, adjoin a site being cleared.—Preservation News, July 1973.

A historic preservation plan will include a detailed survey of the community's architectural and historically valuable properties; it will recommend methods for preserving them and may recommend one or more historic districts to be protected by zoning. If it recommends such districts, it will indicate them on a map. It will discuss the history of the community and its cultural values. It will also examine state or local laws and the ways in which they help or hinder preservation. It will examine certain matters that may be useful for preservation or for the community as a whole, such as the encouragement of tourists or the reviving of trade on run-down commercial streets, and indicate what kind of money might be available for such purposes. If it is a thorough plan, it will include an "action program"—that is, it will tell you not only what ought to be done, but how you may go about doing it. Under the National Historic Preservation Act of 1966, each state is required to prepare a statewide preservation plan. Your local preservation plan should be made part of that.

The trouble about many master plans is that they are made without

Batso Village, New Jersey, site of an early ironworks. — National Register of Historic Places. Photograph by Jon Hackett

public participation and support. A good, workable plan cannot be handed, complete and unalterable, to the public; the public naturally resents hearing that their future has been decided for them by officials and by private-interest groups such as yours. When a master plan is in the air, your organization should be busy getting the public interested in the things you are trying to do—renewing pride in the community's past, showing how handsome its old buildings are, publishing your survey—if you have one ready—illustrating by examples from other communities how commerce and land values can be helped by a thorough preservation program. You have to show, of course, that everyone can benefit in one way or another, that the plan proposed is not a selfish maneuver being imposed on the public. You should get a planning organization that knows how to talk with the public in jargon-free language, that shows respect for suggestions and objections from the public, that knows what the community wants and will pay for. There will be much guesswork in finding such an organization, and of course its bill will have to be met, but with help from public organizations, such as the National Trust, and from public funds, these things should not be impossible.

Perhaps we should repeat that the Tax Reform Act of 1976, as it relates to federally recognized historic districts, offers benefits to property owners and long-term tenants who preserve and restore historic properties well. In presenting your plan to the community, it is wise to stress these benefits.

Finance

Naturally, you need money to acquire property, restore property, print posters, pamphlets, and your survey, and to do the myriad other things your preservation campaign requires: you need money or the equivalent of money.

First, let us run briefly over the equivalents of money. The donation of a facade easement or scenic easement is obviously as good as a cash donation, if the district the property is in is allowed a "higher" or "better" use than that of the present property itself. If a proud homeowner chooses to commit himself and his successors to keeping his house *as a house*, rather than selling it to be demolished for a shopping center, he is foregoing the profits that selling it for a shopping center would bring. True, his taxes are lower, but he is still, in effect, donating money by granting you an easement.

Again, if a lawyer, an architect, or a builder gives you free services because he is a member of your organization, he is saving you the expense of his fees. He may have to charge *something*, but even so you can save a substantial amount. It is good to determine what kind of professional persons might be useful in your organization, especially on your board of directors, and ask them frankly if they are willing to donate their services.

Another equivalent of money is the body of tax incentives a property owner may earn by restoring and preserving a historic property, and the loan or grant money available to him if he does so. The money is in no sense yours, but you can promise it to the property owner by explaining to him how much he can save or gain.

At this point, it is time to explain, briefly, the Tax Reform Act of 1976, which we have already mentioned several times.

The Act, in its Section 2124, covers federal taxation on commercial and other income-producing property of historic value. You will want to check with the Internal Revenue Service for its latest rules on matters of detail, but in general the situation is this:

(1) The tax benefits apply to property owners and to lessees having a lease of thirty years or more, provided that

(2) the property in question is listed as a historic structure in the National Register, individually or as part of a historic district, or is in a state or local historic district certified by the U.S. Secretary of the Interior; provided also that

(3) the property is used in a business or is held for income; and provided, finally, that

(4) the owner or lessee has repaired or remodeled the property in a way that the Secretary of the Interior accepts as keeping or restoring the property's historic character.

(5) There is a choice for the owner or lessee if he has substantially rehabilitated the property: he may amortize (deduct) the cost of rehabilitation over a sixty-month period, or he may depreciate the cost of the property at a faster rate than that applied to nonhistoric buildings.

(6) Furthermore, the party that rehabilitated the property may sell it to a new owner who can benefit from the amortization.

(7) It should be noted that, at present, construction work on the property other than that needed to rehabilitate a historic building is not deductible; neither are general site improvements, nonpermanent walls, furniture, carpeting, and so on.

(8) On the other hand, architect's and engineer's fees, real estate commissions, and various other construction-related costs are deductible; so are the costs of modernization of a historic building required by building codes.

(9) All rehabilitation work must be paid for by mid-1981.

(10) Expenses and losses sustained in demolishing a historic building must be added to the cost of acquiring the land; a replacement building cannot benefit from accelerated depreciation.

(11) The demolition provisions cover *all* buildings in a "registered historic district" unless certification is obtained from the U.S. Secretary of the Interior that a building is not of historic value.

These are the bare essentials of the act and the IRS regulations interpreting it. For further information, write the National Trust for *Preservation and the Tax Reform Act of 1976,* which answers questions in detail, with examples. Write also to the National Register of Historic Places, National Park Service, U.S. Department of the Interior, Washington, D.C. 20240, for more recent rulings and provisions of the Tax Reform Act.

In addition to the federal incentives of the Tax Reform Act, the owner may perhaps benefit locally from incremental taxation. His property, once improved by restoration, may be assessable at a higher figure; but it is possible that the increase in taxation will come gradually, over a number of years, so that the extra burden is not felt all at once. Such a tax policy decision is made by the municipality itself, subject often to state enabling legislation.

Now to the ways your organization can raise and spend money.

A first consideration is the need to acquire a *tax-exempt status* for the organization: obviously, you want to keep the money you raise for your own uses, to avoid any suspicion that you are operating for profit, and to allow donations to be tax-deductible. There are two types of tax-exempt status you can claim, depending on your sources of income. You will probably be appealing to the general public for money, and will therefore want to be registered as a public operating foundation, getting no more than a third of your income, in any one year, from any one source. You will want to claim your exemption under paragraph 501 (C)3 and 509 (a)1 of the Internal Revenue Code. If you do depend primarily on a single income source—though that is generally not a good idea—you will want to claim a so-called "facts and circumstances" exemption, which allows you to get as little as 10 percent of your income from the general public. Contact your attorney on this complex matter.

Perhaps, while we are on the subject of saving money, we should mention the economies of bulk-mailing the literature you send out. Bulk mailing can be done very cheaply by a nonprofit group, provided the instructions of the Post Office regarding addressing and bundling are carried out exactly.

Naturally, your organization can establish a scale of *membership* dues, set up so that no really interested person will feel that he cannot affort to belong, yet allowing for lavish personal gifts. A yearly membership of five dollars or ten dollars is not beyond many people's means, for instance. Normally, this would be called an *active membership*, and would be the cheapest available, unless there were an even cheaper *student membership* for the young. There might also be a *family membership* of about fifteen dollars a year, a *patron membership* of a hundred dollars a year, and a *life membership* of ten thousand dollars or more in a single lifetime payment. Different memberships would be rewarded in different ways: free admission to exhibits and special events, a news bulletin, discounts on things sold by the organization, and some sort of publicity for the members paying the larger amounts.

You must weigh carefully the cost of appealing for members and of

Lucy, the hotel in elephant form, built in the 1880s at Margate, New Jersey. Perhaps other attention-getters of the past — roadhouses, road-side stands, and similar things —should also be preserved, as cultural sidelights. — National Register of Historic Places. Photograph by Jack Boucher, for the Historic American Buildings Survey

giving them services. If you appeal for members by mail, you will generally not get enough dues from new members to make up your printing and mailing costs, *but* once those members renew, paying dues year after year, you will make money. Other expenses to set against membership dues are the cost of printing a newsletter, admitting members to special events free or at a reduced rate, and so on: all the things that reward members for being members but that either cost you money or that reduce the amount of money you can count on from special events.

Membership dues should bring a reliable, steadily increasing flow of money into your treasury, though naturally your daily operations will drain off some of it.

For specific purposes, such as property acquisition and restoration, you will want to have an occasional *capital-fund drive,* a drive to raise money for a specific project or specific kind of project. Here, you are appealing for gifts of money, property, securities, life interests in estates, or bequests—money or its equivalent. Such a drive should be well publicized in the newspapers, on radio and television, and through posters. Welcome contributions of all sizes, and, especially, go after big contributions. It helps to have wealthy board members, in fact, for two reasons: first, because they themselves feel obligated to make large contributions; and second, because they can approach other wealthy persons on a person-to-person basis and persuade them to contribute. If possible, get pledges from such people before the drive is even announced to the public, so that you can say that you are off to a good start. A capital-fund drive should be well-timed (though some say that there is never a perfect time for one), so that donors will feel that they can afford to contribute to it without neglecting other calls on their money. It should be skillfully organized so that every possible source of money is reached.

Of course, be on the lookout for *private gifts* at all times. Remember that, while money is a gift, so are donations of labor and materials, professional services, appropriate furnishings for restoration, and similar things. One further reason to put your organization on a tax-exempt basis is that donations to it will be tax-deductible. Often it is useful to publish a list of specific things you need. People often like to give some specific thing they can consider "theirs." Private gifts are usually solicited on a one-to-one basis; the donor is approached by a friend or business associate. Sometimes persons who have moved away and made good are willing to give money to help the place where they grew up. That was true in Hudson, Ohio (see Chapter 4), and in Winchester, Virginia; in both instances, local boys who had become rich elsewhere conferred great benefits on their home towns. Try to learn of such people, or their descendants, and ask them if they will contribute.

Loans for specific projects are sometimes possible and practical. Perhaps a friend of your organization will lend it money at low interest or no interest at all. And for a specific project, it may be possible to get a bank loan. A bank, especially one with which your organization does business regularly, may be willing to issue a loan secured by a mortgage or by securities put up by some of the members as collateral. If your organization has proven itself to be prudently and responsibly run, and if the project you have in mind seems good for property values in the community, the bank may well agree to a loan on terms easy enough for the organization to repay. Sometimes several banks, in fact, can be interested in putting up portions of the money, each assuming a small amount of the risk. The National Trust for Historic Preservation has a

This city scene from Rochester, New York, might be duplicated by many small towns. Here are mid-nineteenth-century cottages, content to be cottages, and late-nineteenth-century houses that would like to be considered mansions. — National Register of Historic Places. Photograph by Hans Padut

National Historic Preservation Fund, which lends money directly or underwrites bank loans for projects it finds worthy. The fund is limited, however, and is not to be counted on absolutely.

Grants, gifts of money from foundations and trusts for specific projects, are often available. There are in the United States many organizations, large or small, whose purpose is to give away money for causes benefiting the public. Many of these foundations support medical research and other causes that have nothing to do with preservation, but some can help preservationists.

Approach a foundation as you would a bank. Show—

1. that you want the money for a project that will benefit the community (go into detail);
2. that your organization is competent to carry out the project;
3. that you have planned and scheduled the tasks to be done;
4. that you have estimated the cost of each task; and
5. that you have foreseen the kinds of emergencies that might arise and have some way of dealing with them.

In other words, observe the Golden Rule: assume that the foundation you are asking to give you money will want to know the things you would want to know if *you* were lending someone a large amount of money. Be as hardheaded and specific as you can. Be sure, too, to give the foundation credit publicly for the grant if you get it.

Sometimes, of course, the money you raise will have to be applied to one project only; the money will disappear, and a restored building or something similar will appear in its place. But in a community with a good many projects that you might undertake one by one, you should consider establishing a *revolving fund.* In using such a fund, you begin with a generous amount of capital. Some of that you invest in a project—say, the restoration of a house. In time, you rent or sell the house, and the money you get from doing so goes back into the fund until it is needed for another project. This is the revolution of the money: out of the fund, back in, out again, back in, out again, back in, and so on. Such a fund dwindles, in time; it is almost always a loss operation. But before it disappears entirely (except that you should replenish it), it does a great deal of work. Donors like revolving funds, because their money works again and again.

You may be able to get your revolving fund started with a grant through your SHPO from the Heritage, Conservation and Recreation Service of the National Park Service, on a matching basis: that is, the service will put up part of the money you need if you put up the rest of the money *or its equivalent* in property donations.

You may also be able to benefit from some of the programs of the U.S. Department of Housing and Urban Development (HUD), especially those classified as Community Planning and Development. A Community Development Block Grant is sometimes available, though most of the money is intended for cities and highly urbanized areas. The local government can spend it as it pleases to attain three specified goals—housing, environment, and jobs—for lower-income families. Historic preservation is specifically allowable.

Comprehensive Planning Assistance may finance up to two-thirds of a community's comprehensive plan.

Rehabilitation loans are also sometimes available from HUD—a maximum of $27,000 per dwelling unit or $50,000 per nonresidential property. Preference is given to low- and moderate-income persons who show ability to repay and who will use the money to bring buildings up to building-code and other code standards.

There may soon also be specific Historic Preservation Loans, guaranteed by the Federal Housing Administration (FHA) of HUD. These are made by private, FHA-insured lending institutions for properties that are either on the National Register or that are eligible for inclusion on the

Now and then, a good bandstand survives, in a village green or small-town park. This unusually elaborate and well-preserved one is in Belleville, Ohio. — National Register of Historic Places. Photograph by Larry Alan Beers

Register and that are to be used for residential purposes. Loans may be up to $15,000 per dwelling unit (no more than $45,000 per building), at an interest rate of not over 12 percent. Up to fifteen years can be taken in repaying. Ask your bank or local HUD office for details.

Legislation is now on the books authorizing HUD's "Livable Cities" program, matching grants for municipalities and nonprofit groups for projects improving the quality of life. Contact HUD for application forms.

Let us go back, for a moment, to the subject of *events*. Special events not only tell the public that your preservation movement is alive and well; they are also good ways of raising capital. Many towns have festivals, based on local history or the present-day life of the town. Winchester, Virginia, a center for the growing and processing of apples, has an Apple Festival every spring. West Middletown, a village in Washington County, Pennsylvania, has an Apple Pie Festival; Washington County itself has a Covered Bridge Festival. San Antonio, Texas, has a four-day annual festival that raises over a quarter-million dollars. Natchez, Mississippi, has an old-house tour, admissions from which are divided between the preservation organization and the house owners, who use their part to help maintain their magnificent old homes. Once you have a few interested people and know what there is about your community that the outside world might like to see, consider a festival very seriously.

Conclusion

In this chapter we have tried to cover complicated subjects in a few words. Much of what we have said is (we hope) simple common sense, while the rest is less obvious. Much is definitely within the province of the lawyer, the banker, or the architect. The bibliography at the back of this book may be of help in suggesting other books covering specific subjects more thoroughly.

3
Preserving a Property

These are a few hints on how to save an actual property. The authors, in putting them together, have been thinking in most instances of fairly large buildings, and it is obvious that a log cabin or a tract of rural land would sometimes require different procedures.

Perhaps this is as good a place as any to talk about the many kinds of property that might be worth saving in a small town or a rural community. Preservationists consider that *anything* physical, including open land, can be mutilated or destroyed unless deliberate care is taken that it be preserved. In the scenic Green Springs area of Virginia, far from cities, the state almost succeeded in building a huge penitentiary that would have marred the beauty of the area. In town, a handsome old courthouse may outlive its original purpose and be demolished before preservationists can get a binding agreement to save it; such an incident happened in Illinois a few years ago.

The preservationist has a heavy burden of proof on his shoulders in areas where historic preservation is unfamiliar. An appeal to sentiment is seldom enough, and the need for museums is limited. "Adaptive use" is the way of preservation today. A convincing argument for preservation must rest on objective data showing that the property, secured by a covenant, will remain useful in the community and will continue to pay its way, though very possibly in a role that its builders never imagined. Up to a point, one needs imagination in thinking of the future of the property; beyond that point, one needs to be thoroughly objective, talking dollars and cents, weighing public demand for the kind of space the property has. An old house, for example: shall it continue to house one family? Shall it be made into apartments? Shall it become offices? Shall it be an old-fashioned "dining rooms" type of restaurant? Or a small railroad station: shops, perhaps? Or, again, a restaurant? Or a headquarters for the Red Cross or other community service agencies? An old factory is often regarded as ugly because it *is* a factory, or is regarded as a souvenir of an ugly past that the town wants to forget. Yet a factory building is strongly constructed, well lighted, and has open space that can be divided up in many ways. Often, it is a very handsome building, too, once you get the dirt of the years off it and clear away shabby additions to the basic structure. You may end up with a stately building that can be made into apartments, offices, a school, a shopping center: all these things have been done to industrial buildings with great success. A church is a challenge, yet it is a familiar sight in the community, one that would be missed; if it cannot go on being a place of worship, perhaps it can become a public hall of some kind, or even a house. A warehouse, like a factory, may be able to house any of a number of functions. A row of little stores may be joined together to form one big store. Do not let ordinary habits of thought dominate you as you look at properties that you would miss should they be lost.

Here are some points to consider:

Do a superficial inspection of the property in question and begin to

A drab commercial street in Medina, Ohio, with inharmonious signs and infelicitous attempts at modernization. — National Trust for Historic Preservation

imagine a future for it. If it is a building, note how it is being used and the condition it appears to be in. Does it seem to be paying its way, to be fully and well occupied, or is it shabby, deserted, and misused? How does its structural condition look? Do you find sagging or bulging brick walls, boards under the eaves coming loose, broken windows, or a grave need of new paint? (If you are thinking of buying, the shabbiness may be a good sign, an indication of an owner who might be put in a selling mood.) Will restoration be too much for you to tackle? Is the shabbiness just a surface matter, or does it look as if there is major structural damage? (Be optimistic, however, in considering what you may be able to do; the state of the building, and your resources for restoring it, are not to be underestimated if you are going to be effective as preservationists.)

Rehabilitated and modernized sympathetically, this Medina, Ohio, street appears far more pleasing to the eye than it did before renovation. Commercial buildings display signs that are individual, yet compatible, and ground-floor modernization is consistent in appearance from shop to shop. No attempt was made to introduce fake Victorian windows or decorations; participating merchants, agreed that the old storefronts were gone, approved new construction that would achieve architectural harmony. — National Trust for Historic Preservation

How might the building be used? What might the community need—housing, more shops, a museum, a library, a place with tourist appeal? For what uses might the size of the property, the size of the building and the distribution of its windows and doors, be sufficient? Try to guess at demands that the property might meet.

What is the future of the property's environment? Is the neighborhood a shabby, hard-to-reach one, or is it easily accessible and pleasant? Is it residential, industrial, commercial? Are there zoning restrictions on land use? Are there nearby improvement projects in the offing? Will there be new building or road construction? Think of your property in the setting it will probably have. Get some first impressions, in other words, but remember that you will have to get hard data on these matters if you go on with the project.

Like churches, courthouses help to make each town different from all others. Usually, the courthouse is in a block by itself, surrounded by a lawn, to emphasize its importance to the government of the county and the life of the town. Thus, the setting for the Wooster, Ohio, courthouse, shown here, is unusual: it is in a business block, where other buildings lend it the effect of being much larger than it actually is. Preservationists face a special challenge in dealing with older courthouses. If such a structure cannot really function, in its old age, as the seat of an expanded county government, does it have to be torn down? Perhaps it can be adapted to other uses, commercial or public, as has been done with some city halls. —Mary Means

Decide how to handle the situation. Remember that even a property in fine shape is not necessarily a secure property. With regard to open land, developers sometimes find it useful to buy early and cheaply, and allow farming or other activities to continue on the land for a while. Doing so avoids organized public protests until the developers are ready to clear and build. And a building owner can always sell out if the price if right, even though he keeps his property in good condition while he owns it. Make early contact with a property owner and find out what he is likely to do. Will he grant you or sell you a facade or scenic easement, guaranteeing preservation of what the public sees? Or, on the other hand, will you have to buy or lease?

One thing that you can buy, if your present resources are scant, is time.

The board-and-batten house, with vertical moldings covering the siding, has been used in the United States since the 1830s. Here is an 1858 example from Fort Dalles, Oregon, that looks like the first ones, built two decades earlier near the Hudson River. Such houses, which take on a bold, striped effect in the sunlight, are among the best-looking we have ever built and should be carefully preserved. — Oregon Historical Society. Photograph by Walter Boychuk

An *option to purchase* can often be arranged. On condition that the property is left unaltered in the meantime, you pay the owner for the right to buy the building within a certain period, usually a few months. This gives you a chance to raise some capital funds and gives the owner some profit in addition to any other money that he is getting all along. Sometimes the option money can be deducted from the selling price; try to make that a part of the agreement. Of course, unless you have a portion of the purchase money the owner demands when the option period is over, you have no further deal with the owner, and the option money is his.

If you are confident that you can come up with the money, you can often arrange a *sales contract,* by which you obligate yourself absolutely

A Mormon co-operative store of 1870 at Ephraim, Utah. Fortunately, stores of almost every size have a chance of remaining useful if the economic life of a community is good. In adapting them to new uses, the owner or tenant should try to preserve and recondition the original ornament and detailing, throw away any later, cheap remodeling, add new signs or other items needed for business in a harmonious way, always working to avoid "cuteness" or fake history. — National Register of Historic Places

to buy the property at the end of a certain time. The term of such a contract may be a month or six months. Expect the purchase price to be higher than it would be if you bought the property at once, since the owner will have it on his hands longer.

In getting a *mortgage,* see if you can get one from the property owner. Doing so can avoid a large equity investment or down-payment.

You can often arrange a *lease,* and sometimes its terms can include an option to purchase when the lease runs out.

Whatever, you do, get a *title search,* making sure that you have the whole bundle of rights that comes with the property. It would be unpleasant to find out, for example, that you did not have the mineral rights and that a strip mine or an oil well could be started on your property early some morning.

Do some careful study on the condition of the property. Find an architect, engineer, architectural historian, landscape architect, or other consultants, according to circumstances, to inspect the present condition of the property thoroughly. Do that as soon as you have access to the property and as soon as you have the means of paying consultants' fees. You may be thinking of tackling the impossible (though you should lean toward optimism). Find consultants who are used to working with historic properties, because they will not be immediately discouraged by unfamiliar building techniques, building code violations, peculiar structural conditions, and so on. A professional who is used to working only with new structures may feel helpless in the presence of heavy masonry walls that are bulging in places, or other features that time has affected but that may not be in as bad condition as they seem.

At times, be prepared to pay your consultants more than the usual rate. An old building, especially, has to be gone over carefully, foot by foot, and some way found of telling the contractor how to handle many problems of detail. It is only fair that the consultants be paid for the extra time such a process takes.

Do some careful study of the demands the building might fulfill. Try to unite two things: public demand for certain kinds of space in certain parts of the community, and the ways in which your building can supply part of the demand. Have you a scenic tract of land by a river, and does the community need a park? Would a park destroy the character you find valuable about the land? Or could it be the kind of park that would make appreciative use of the open meadows, the handsome old trees that you want to preserve? Is there a demand for housing, and would your old woodworking or textile mill make good apartments? Might professional persons, a lawyer and a dentist, for example, be interested in rooms on opposite sides of the center hall in your mansion, with apartments above? Sound out friends in the real estate business, and possibly public officials, to see what the community's building-space needs are.

As you get information on the demand for space, have your consultant draw up tentative plans, consider building codes, explore the possibilities for financing, and so on, so that you have practical schemes to offer: not plans worked out in every detail, of course—details come later—but plans specific enough to show that the property you own or hope to own can meet the demands the community has for space.

Inspect the neighborhood thoroughly and try to predict its future. Find

Street scene in Galesburg, Illinois, around 1925. The building, dating from about 1910, is made of tapestry brick; trim is stone or terra cotta. The lower store windows have neatly furled awnings, ready to roll down to protect the stock from sunlight and to encourage shopping. The upper windows appear to be of ribbed glass, which would bend sun rays and send them further into the store. The large public clock in front was a genteel advertising device popular in that era. The elaborate lamp-post, though not very practical as a way of lighting the street, was at least good-looking. — Galesburg Public Library, Galesburg, Illinois

out, by all means, about major construction or demolition that will change the character of the neighborhood. Be sure that the property you are after will not be condemned by eminent domain. (Though remember, always, that if you can get your property on the National Register of Historic Places, it will be very hard for others to get federal help for a public project that will injure it.) Think of whether the public will want to come to your neighborhood for the purposes you have in mind. Are there, or will there be, similar attractions there? If not, does it matter? Is your neighborhood dreary, dangerous-looking, or pleasant? Is it out of the way, or handy to places where the public often goes? What about streets and public transportation?

In thinking about the future of the neighborhood, think of the effect your project may have on it; it may well have an important good influence, especially if the neighborhood itself is basically all right.

Remember that a deteriorating neighborhood may be "red-lined" by lending institutions—that is, it may be looked upon as a place where the

Galesburg, Illinois, around 1895: a small town, with the pompous and rather tall buildings of a town, yet, in places, still a bit like a village. Plenty of trees. — Galesburg Public Library, Galesburg, Illinois

building's market value will not serve as sufficient collateral for a loan. Again, HUD offers some assistance to such neighborhoods, and you should contact the Neighborhood Commission at HUD for information. It is important to recognize early that, in dealing with a decayed area, you will have to raise private funds, obtain personal signatures of substantial people as collateral, or find HUD or municipal assistance for restoration costs.

Check building codes, zoning laws, and other ordinances. Be sure that your proposed plans will be lawful. Pay careful attention to life safety codes and handicapped-access laws, which may demand expensive alterations.

Check FHA regulations, current policies of lending institutions, and so on, to be sure that you can get the conventional financing you need. Financing may be difficult.

Once you have in mind a use or range of uses for your property, make as careful an estimate as you can of income and expenditure, so that you know whether the property will pay for itself as you propose to use it. If you remain the owner or lessee, you will have to know whether your

How not to modernize Main Street: tear down stores and substitute bare pavements; tear off ornament and substitute bare, windowless walls. — National Trust for Historic Preservation. Photograph by James L. Ballard, for the Main Street Project, 1978

project will have to be subsidized, and to what extent; if you are leasing or selling to others, they will want to be sure that they will not lose out.

Think, we repeat, about grant money. Some private foundations and trusts, and some government organizations, too, are set up to grant (i.e., give) or to lend money at low interest to support worthy preservation causes. Look for such organizations and present them with facts and figures. Convince them that a public demand exists for what you are trying to do and that you have the ability and willingness to supply the demand in an efficient, economical way. Go to such organizations as you would a banker; they may not be after a profit, just as you will not be, but they will want to know that their money is being spent sensibly. Go into detail as far as you can without having the gift of prophecy. If you get grant money, give the granting organization public credit for its help. Be prepared, later, to report unflinchingly on your success or failure.

Get public officials interested, as early as possible, in your project. That accomplishes several things. First, if your project seems likely to be

Typical, old-fashioned store buildings, often ignored. But look at the sign lettering and the orderly, well-proportioned fronts. A builders' supply house in Madison, Indiana.—National Trust for Historic Preservation. Photograph by James L. Ballard, for the Main Street Project, 1978

popular, you can get their verbal support for it. Second, since your plans will have to be examined for conformity to the building code and other ordinances, you may be able to get them approved, stage by stage, as they develop, so that, by the time you are in working drawings, the plans will be fully approved. This saves you time—and, in our inflationary time, money—through an early start on actual construction. Officials may also be persuaded to approve solutions to problems that go outside the letter of the law, if these are not dangerous or obnoxious. Third, you may be able to persuade officials to improve paving, lighting, and services in the area of your project. And fourth, if your community has federal revenue-sharing money, some of it may be allocated to help your project.

Get everybody interested; make the project a popular one, for the following reasons:

- you get the officials behind you;
- you convince lending institutions, foundations that might offer

A very wide Main Street in Madison, Indiana. This is a good-looking Main Street, too, aside from the distractions provided by signs, lamp-posts, and wires. Here, a community master plan might arrange a truce in the war of advertising, light the pedestrian and the motorist safely, and tell the latter when to stop and where to go with considerably less clutter. A master plan is worth the attempt if a more beautiful town can be achieved as a result.—National Trust for Historic Preservation. Photograph by James L. Ballard, for the Main Street Project, 1978

grants, and individuals that might contribute that you are doing a valuable public service;

- you attract those to whom you will want to sell or rent;
- you raise the morale of the community, and enliven its spirits.

Sometimes (check local and state laws) you can issue special "goodwill" securities for a project, borrowing at a low interest or no interest at all. The honor of buying such securities can make up for the customary profit, if the buyers are given credit. Always, if anyone is especially generous, be prepared to publicize his or her name.

When you know that you are going to restore or remodel, get a good contractor; do it as soon as possible. Try to find a person who has had experience in restoration work, or who is willing to learn new methods. Put him in contact with your architect or other consultant before working drawings are made. Working drawings are expensive, and may not be necessary for every one of the many little details that crop up in restoring an old property. If the contractor can do a good job without them, you will save money. Encourage the contractor to gather a team of workmen who enjoy the challenge that an out-of-the-way job like this brings; such workmen exist.

If the job is a small one, consider being your own contractor. The cares are greater, but if you know what to do, the cost is less, since the contractor's profit is eliminated.

All this is very general and it will be very useful to have an architect, a builder, a lawyer, and a banker or some similar combination of professionals on your board to help guide your organization in carrying out a project. In general, once again, be optmistic. Most of the preservation triumphs have been accomplished by people who have thought about what they *could* do rather than what they couldn't. You are undertaking something out of the ordinary, so try to imagine out-of-the-ordinary ways of doing it.

4
Case Histories

✦

These are a few of the experiences that preservationists have had in attempting to save the historic character of a town or a village. These experiences are interesting, we think, because they show the intricacies a preservation effort may demand, the various hazards preservationists may encounter, as well as the techniques they can employ.

We begin with a rather sad case: a Connecticut village known as a gem but whose Main Street has an uncertain future. Then we go on to happier stories.

Essex, Connecticut
W. C. K.

The importance of beginning a historic preservation effort early is being felt, belatedly, in the village of Essex, Connecticut. Situated five miles up the Connecticut River, this village enjoys a superb natural setting among wooded hills. Until the late nineteenth century, Essex and the other river ports in the area prospered from commercial shipping and shipbuilding, but declined thereafter. Railroads began to carry the coastal freight, while a sandbar and a railroad bridge shut out the ocean-going vessels that might have turned the river shores into a string of seaports and industrial sites. Comparative stagnation preserved both the landscape and the Colonial, Early Federal, and Greek Revival houses that Essex citizens had built in days of prosperity.

Beginning around 1920, yachtsmen began to enter the river in large numbers, and in the course of things discovered the old port, whose tree-lined Main Street extended down a peninsula between two coves. Property was cheap, and outsiders, particularly New Yorkers, began to buy and restore the old houses of Main Street and the adjacent streets for summer or retirement homes. Enough of a change had taken place by

1933 that, in that year, the Essex Yacht Club was founded. In the mid-1960s, the village was looking its very best, its houses bright with paint, its lawns and gardens beautifully tended. There was some shabbiness, but the course of things was against its remaining. There seemed no reason to have more than the conventional land-use zoning law that was enacted in 1964; a proposal for historic-district zoning, made around the same time, was defeated, and a similar proposal of 1974 led to little more than an unpublished architectural survey.

As regards preservation, the citizens of Essex fall roughly into three classes. There are the old families, some of whose names are centuries old in the region. They are proud of their town, but generally opposed to any restriction on disposing of their properties as they wish. There are the recent settlers, who have invested hope, energy, and money in their homes and who want to ensure that the semirural peace and beauty of the region is maintained. Finally, there is the business community, which ministers to a variety of customers. Most of Essex's shops are for locals, rather than transients such as yachtsmen or tourists. The things they

View of Main Street, Essex, Connecticut, around 1900. The street goes down the center of a peninsula jutting into the Connecticut River. The building in the center, rear, is the Steamboat Dock, a way landing for the New York-Hartford night boat. —Dahlstrom Collection

sell—prosaic things, like food and hardware; fancy things, like imported kitchenware or carpets—are purchased mostly by people who live in the lower Connecticut Valley. The staple goods are mostly found at the head of Main Street in buildings that—these days, at least—seldom have special architectural worth. Many of them were Victorian, once, but have been cheaply Colonialized with imitation clapboarding of vinyl or aluminum. Along the center and at the foot of Main are the more elegant shops, mixed with old houses still lived in. Some of the old houses have been gutted inside for business or commercial space, while new buildings, annexes, and possibly some adaptations of stables and other outbuildings have helped accommodate the continuing demand for such space. By the river shore, the character changes, for here yachts are sold, maintained, supplied, and stored, and their occupants are accommodated. The architecture here tends to be plain, frankly industrial or modern in character, continuing a maritime tradition centuries old. Yachting is catered to, partly because it is a favorite sport in Essex, partly because it is so important to the economy. As to the tourists, most Essex people, including business people, regard them as more trouble than

The Ebenezer Hayden house, Essex, Connecticut, built in 1778. Larger than most Main Street houses in Essex, but typical in its quiet good taste. — Dahlstrom Collection

they are worth. Though not received hostilely, tourists are not catered to, in most shops, and at present are probably not very important in the over-all village economy.

Essex celebrated the bicentennial with a pageant and a concluding ceremony that showed the morale and collective spirit of the community; but in the following summer, an incident occurred that gave some citizens a shock. There had been a plot of trees and shrubs at one Main Street corner, admired for its beauty, and suddenly the plant life was cleared away to give place for a new commercial building, a Georgian pastiche out of harmony with the authentic architecture of the street. The action made people conscious of what they had probably been dimly feeling, that Main Street was getting too commercial, and was being spoiled. Other complaints came to the surface: rowdyism around the bars and in the town park (where an old house had been) angered some; tourist buses roaring down the street annoyed others. Furthermore, there was no legal obstruction whatever to the defacement or demolition of a historic building, so long as its replacement conformed to the land-use zoning; and much of that zoning, on Main Street, was commercial.

Since historic-district zoning had met with apathy, preservationists did

The Griswold Inn, Essex, Connecticut, said to have been begun in 1776. A restaurant and hotel with a long tradition, but clad, these days, in vinyl siding and "shutters." —Richard S. Lovelace, Jr.

the only thing they could: they requested that the Zoning Commission consider a major change, on central Main Street, from commercial to residential. That would be of some help in protecting the old houses and in maintaining a balance—recognized by the preservationists as desirable—between the two uses. Business properties would be labeled "nonconforming," but allowed to remain. The commission agreed to a moratorium of several months on new business construction while the public temper was tested.

At the time of this writing, the outcome of the belated preservation movement remains uncertain. It may succeed, but much damage, hardly reversible, has already been done. Victorian architecture, regarded as expendable, has been shaved to surfaces that vinyl siding can easily cover. Mandatory parking spaces for houses converted to commercial uses have covered portions of back yards. New construction, according to a new ordinance, has to be set back from the sidewalk for fire safety—almost all construction, new or old, is frame—and this violates the prevailing tradition. And, as in many small-town (and big-town) situations, disputes over principles have sometimes taken on a note of personal squabbling. Had the moment been seized at which the fortui-

The Starkey house, Essex, Connecticut, 1793. Covered with aluminum imitation siding and made over, inside, into shops and offices. — Richard S. Lovelace, Jr.

tous beauty of Essex might have been fully preserved by a code that integrated considerations of amenity, balance of commerce and residential use, fire protection, and any others, the village would have been the better for it. The squabbling—doubtless inevitable—would have been dispensed with, and the village would have had more security today about what it wants to be and how it should look. The best time for that would probably have been about seventeen years ago.

Hudson, Ohio
Patricia Eldridge, Hudson Heritage Association

The preservation of the village of Hudson, in the Western Reserve section of Ohio, has been a result of a variety of factors, both calculated and accidental. Not the least of these was a little poverty at the right time.

Hudson was founded in 1800 by a group of Connecticut settlers led by David Hudson of Goshen, who gave the town his name. It was a prosperous enough settlement, from the beginning, to warrant a daily stage coach and mail three times a week. In 1826, it was chosen as the site for Western Reserve College (dubbed by its founders the Yale of the West), and the resulting bustle and activity further spurred the town's growth. Much of the architecture for which Hudson is known dates from the twenty-five-year period after the founding of the college.

In the late 1840s, the Cleveland and Pittsburgh Railroad was completed as far as Hudson, with a spur to Akron opening soon after. Business boomed, and the population almost doubled. New industries moved in, and the entire town contracted railroad fever. Three new railroad companies were formed, and the people of Hudson mortgaged houses and invested life savings to buy railroad stock. With the Panic of 1857, the paper railroads were wiped out, and so were the fortunes of many of the businesses and people of Hudson.

Construction did not entirely stop, however. There are a number of very good buildings of the 1860s and 1870s in the village. The college, after all, made the town the hub of intellectual activity in the northeastern part of Ohio. Then, in 1882, the directors of the college accepted a bequest that imposed the condition that it move to Cleveland and become Western Reserve University. With the college went the last of Hudson's dreams of glory, and a good many of its citizens, too. By 1900, the population was slightly more than seven hundred, less than it had been seventy years before. An embezzlement scandal involving the local bank and a disastrous fire that wiped out an entire business block facing the green in 1892 added to the gloom. During the last twenty years of the nineteenth century, there was very little in the way of new construction or remodeling of buildings. Those that might otherwise have been demolished or altered as unfashionable or past their prime were retained simply for lack of funds. Thus, when the first planned preservation effort began, some seventy years ago, there was a good deal of the old village left.

In the first years of this century, a local-boy-made-good returned to his old home town and built an estate on land within the village limits.

Though James W. Ellsworth had been born in Hudson in 1849, he had left as a teen-ager and had made a fortune in coal in Chicago and Pennsylvania. When he returned to his birthplace and saw the desolation—the storefronts abandoned, the former college buildings grim and empty, with broken windows and unhinged doors—Ellsworth determined that Hudson should become a "model village." On October 20, 1907, he unveiled his plan to the village council. He, James Ellsworth, would build for the town an electric generating station, a sewage-treatment plant, and a city water system capable, with later extensions that could be made as needed and paid for by the village, of serving a population of at least 5,000. For its part, however, the village must agree to nine conditions. They must, for instance, remove all overhead wiring and install it in conduits under the streets. They must plant elm trees on both sides of all streets. They must prohibit street-railway cars, and they must establish laws preventing the sale of liquor within the town. He also directed that a corporation be formed to buy the lands and buildings of the former Western Reserve College (which later became Western Reserve Academy). On December 10, 1907, Mr. Ellsworth's terms were accepted by the village council.

Ellsworth was not always loved by the citizens of the town he wished to make a model community. He was exacting and demanding, and insisted that things be done his own way. There was organized opposition to his policies, and the village actually elected an opposition mayor and repudiated Ellsworth's generosity at one time. There is no question, however, that Hudson would not be the town it is today were it not for its controversial benefactor.

The fame of the Model Town plan introduced Hudson to a new phenomenon: the commuter. In the 1920s, Cleveland and Akron business and professional men began to move into town with their families, taking advantage of what was then excellent train service. At this time an ambitious scheme for a planned community in Hudson was developed by S. N. Kleinman. It provided for a golf course, Tudor style clubhouse, and several lakes, around which ample lots on curving streets were clustered. The village annexed the area and put in sewers and street lighting. Were it not for the depression of the 1930s, in which Kleinman and his financier failed, Hudson might well have become another Shaker Heights. As it was, Hudson settled back into limbo. Economic growth was all but halted, and storefronts again stood empty in the village.

Even the postwar boom did not reach the village until the early 1950s, with the completion of the Ohio Turnpike near the north outskirts of town and the coming of the General Motors Euclid Division plant in the southern end of the township. Then began a growth that threatened to push a country village and its surrounding township into suburbanization. In 1950 the population of the village was 1,538 and of the outlying township 1,339. Ten years later, the village had grown by 900 residents and the township had nearly doubled (2,539). Moreover, in the quarter-century between 1950 and 1975, the village population multiplied 2.8 times, and that of the township quadrupled. Scarcely more than half the streets on the map today existed twenty-five years ago. The first shopping center, the first apartment building, the first strip development—all have appeared in the same span of time.

With mounting pressures and problems, the Village Council commissioned the planning firm of Ladislau Segoe and Associates to write a master plan for Hudson, which was presented in 1957. The provisions made for by-pass roads and street extensions in the plan were enthusiastically received, and it was the first plan to propose an architectural board of review. However, it also suggested that four of the five blocks of the green at the village center be eventually obliterated and that public buildings be constructed on the sites. (The Fire Department had already used one of them for its new facilities in 1954.) The orientation of the brick stores on the west side of the green was to be reversed, so that the major access would be from the parking area in the rear. The plan also proposed that the row of early nineteenth-century wooden buildings just north of the green be replaced by a parking lot. As Rebecca Rogers says, in her *Hudson, Ohio: An Architectural and Historical Study,* the plan would have destroyed the function of the greens as the town's commercial and social center, leaving only a small patch of grass and trees. She blames the faults of the plan on its tendency to view Hudson as a "typical" town—one that would have to provide for all of its citizens' needs—disregarding the proximity of neighboring towns and commercial developments. Certainly the plan was influenced by the vehicular obsession of the fifties and sixties, when extensive construction of multilane highways, with their sprawling "cloverleaf" access ramps, held high priority.

Fortunately, only parts of the Segoe plan were implemented, and the proposals for the area around the green were virtually ignored. One individual who was a member of the council at that time has since said that the community felt that Segoe could not possibly know what the people of Hudson wanted, since the plan included some proposals that Hudsonians simply could not agree to. Moreover, the plan would have required the co-operation of the village, the township, and the merchants—who were evidently unwilling to "turn around and face backward."

While the community's thoughts were turned to planning for the future, several brave and caring individuals were involved in saving parts of the past. An English teacher at the academy managed to persuade the trustees of that institution to retain and restore North College, one of the original college buildings. A descendant of David Hudson saved the Hudson homestead (1806) by baking and selling bread and serving tea from the house. One of the township trustees, who still hold title to the green, singlehandedly blocked several attempts to encroach upon the area for parking and road widening. A copy of the original deed of gift from Hudson to the township was found, printed, framed, and hung in the trustees' chambers as a reminder.

An organized effort to preserve historic buildings and maintain the small-town character of the village was finally mounted in 1962. As usual, it was born of crisis. The local bank, which James Ellsworth had helped to reorganize, had become a branch of a large Akron banking firm. The building it occupied was originally the Brewster store, built in 1831 and reputed to be the oldest extant commercial building in the Western Reserve. It stood at a central location on the green. The bank felt cramped in the small building and wanted drive-in facilities. Although no announcement was made, their plans to replace the Brewster store with a more modern structure became known.

The threat to this important building brought the community together. Those who had worked alone and those who had never been active before were drawn into a collective effort. Everyone who could possibly be of influence was asked to put pressure on the bank and write to the local papers in support of preservation. Large depositors talked to local bank officials. An informal group calling itself Keep Hudson Beautiful was formed to co-ordinate the efforts.

Finding little satisfaction locally, however, two concerned women went to Washington to talk to their congressman and to the National Trust. The Akron newspaper was persuaded to send a reporter along with them, and thus their trip was guaranteed good coverage in the bank's headquarters city. Says one of the women, "We pointed out to the Congressman that Ohio had very few acres of federally funded park lands, and that Hudson, with its Green, its architecture, and its country town feeling, served the same purpose as a park for nearby communities." The congressman gave them moral support, introduced them to other congressmen, and had his picture taken with them for the Akron paper.

One of the women explains: "You must realize that this was 1962. We were starting out from ground zero. Mr. Ayers was for us, but he didn't know what to do, and we didn't know what to ask him to do. But we felt that if a Congressman would receive us and not laugh at wanting to save an old building, if he would appear with us in the paper, it would give us a certain amount of clout locally."

At the National Trust, the women were promised a consultant. Helen Duprey Bullock, then editor of *Preservation News*, arrived in Hudson for the annual ice cream social on the green and for a large meeting held at one of the academy buildings, where she was to speak. It was at this meeting that the Hudson Heritage Association was officially founded as Hudson's preservation organization. Its first order of business was the salvation of the Brewster store. Most of its officers and founding members, in fact, had taken an active part in the bank controversy.

Whether because of pressure or persuasion, the bank decided to retain the building. Once again, no announcement was made, but work soon began on the structural reinforcement of the interior and on a small drive-in wing, which was added to the rear.

The Heritage Association, however, did not rest long on its laurels. Other buildings were appearing on the Most-Threatened list. The Rufus Nutting house on the academy campus had been condemned. One of the Hudson Heritage board members, a local architect, donated his time and talents, and the academy was persuaded to restore it for use as a faculty housing. HHA was also instrumental in saving an early nineteenth-century inn which, although outside the township, was considered to be particularly important. It stood in the path of a new highway, and the time that the highway department had allotted for purchase bids had already elapsed with no buyers coming forth. Demolition bids were about to be let. At HHA's urging, the local highway superintendent agreed to keep the bids open for another two weeks. An all-out publicity campaign was waged, and a buyer willing to move the house was found in the nick of time.

A marking program was also undertaken for important Hudson buildings, to include extensive and meticulous research. The first HHA marker, appropriately enough, was awarded to the Brewster store.

As well as saving valuable buildings, Hudson Heritage Association was founded to maintain the integrity of the green and its surrounding area; to encourage for new buildings use of the same good taste that characterized the structures put up by Hudson's founders; to encourage the preservation and planting of trees; and to co-operate with other organizations to the end of a well-integrated community in keeping with its tradition as an early settlement of the Western Reserve.

Because of diligence and watchfulness (HHA members were assigned to monitor meetings of every public body), and because of the dedication of members of the Village Council, the Township Trustees, and the Planning Commission, as well as the concern of civic groups such as the Hudson Garden Club, great strides were taken toward these goals.

The Garden Club had been planting trees and shrubs in public places for some years, and had provided equipment for maintenance of plant materials and the spraying of diseased elms. Its activities were paid for by an annual Home-and-Garden Tour. It had long advocated a Tree Commission for the town, even before a study by a firm of landscape architects (which the Garden Club hired) recommended a paid official responsible for trees and plantings. (The Hudson Heritage Association had discussed urging a Tree Commission on the Village Council.)

HHA was already involved in tree-preservation efforts when it learned that the state proposed to widen Route 303, one of two major arteries through town. The widening would not only have altered the character of Route 303 from the appearance of a village street to that of an improved highway; it would also have necessitated the removal of and ensured the death of the priceless old trees that lined its borders. Alarmed, a delegation went to interview the local deputy director of the state highway department. While they were looking at maps, he pointed out, incidentally, that county highway officials were proposing an extension of Barlow Road to accommodate traffic from the General Motors plant, very similar to the bypass for Route 303 that had been proposed by the Segoe Plan. Next, the delegation approached the county. It suggested that, if the state could be persuaded to build an Alternate 303 that would relieve the county of the expense of the Barlow Road project, the county might perhaps take over maintenance of the present Route 303, effecting a swap. The county official didn't see why not. The swap was proposed to the state highway director in Columbus, and the concern of Hudson about the widening of 303 was eloquently expressed. According to a contemporary newspaper account, the director agreed to pursue the question of the swap with the county, and as much as promised a temporary, if not permanent, freeze on the widening.

In 1967, the efforts of the Garden Club and Hudson Heritage to secure a permanent official to see to the planting and preservation of trees finally resulted in a paid tree commissioner. His duties have been expanded over the years, and he has been greatly aided by a land-use plan, commissioned in 1971 and referred to locally as the Knight-and-Stollar

Plan. Its primary purpose is as a guide for the park board, the school district, and the tree commissioner on the use and development of open spaces.

Certainly one of the most important accomplishments of the Hudson Heritage Association during its early years was the formation of an architectural board of review. This, suggested in the Segoe Plan, had been enthusiatically approved but never brought into being, and there was growing concern about the type and amount of construction going on in the village and on the erstwhile farmlands surrounding it. At the first general meeting after its inception, HHA unanimously endorsed the creation of an architectural board of review, to be established as quickly as possible. A task force was appointed to gather information from, and copies of ordinances concerning, architectural boards anywhere in the country. As one of its first directors later put it, the organization gathered the necessary information and put it into the proper hands.

The right hands, in this instance, were those of a director of Hudson Heritage and member of both the Planning Commission and the Village Council. By spring of 1963, an ordinance had been introduced, and by October it had become a part of the established code of the Village of Hudson. It created a five-member, unsalaried Architectural Review Board—later expanded to seven—which had to approve any plans before the town's building inspector could issue a building permit, either for new construction or for alterations or additions.

The purpose of the board was to maintain the property values of the town by preserving its character, and those of the neighbors of any property by preventing inappropriate structures or additions. Specifically, it was to guard against "look-alike subdivisions." No building was to resemble in more than two of the following aspects any neighboring structure within three lots on either side or across the street: size and shape; roof style and pitch; relative position of windows, doors, and chimneys; relative position of major design features such as garages, porches, and so on; and major exterior building materials. Appeals could be taken to the town's Board of Zoning Appeals.

The "look-alike" clause has seldom been called upon, perhaps because it is so specific that builders have little difficulty avoiding the letter of the law. In other respects, the power of the board to accomplish its purposes is rather vague. It has ordinarily tried persuasion, bolstered at times by procedures provided for in the ordinance that, if carried out in full, can cause a substantial delay, if not a final denial, of a building permit. Builders, it seems, are always in a hurry, and can often be nudged in the right direction if that means that time can be saved. The Architectural

Board in Hudson, however, prefers rather to persuade by the logic of its own experience.

It prefers not to reject applications, but rather to meet with the applicant and to explain and suggest ways in which the building may be made more attractive and/or more compatible with the Hudson character. On the positive side, that approach tends to avoid confrontations and maintain a workable atmosphere. At times, the builder may even be saved some expense: a plain wooden lintel is not only more in keeping with Hudson architecture, but a good deal less costly than a structural-foam, broken-pediment detail. On the negative side, however, this method is apt to result in a piecemeal approach.

Recently, the board has been aided in its persuasion by the adoption of uniform architectural criteria for the Village of Hudson. The criteria attempt to establish guidelines for new construction, based on a detailed study of the architectural character of the village. Because the state's conflict-of-interest laws have been interpreted to mean that no person liable to appear before the board may be a member of it, it contains no practicing architects. Therefore, it seemed most important to establish written standards, scientifically reached, to reduce the chance of criticism of board action on the basis of arbitrariness of either taste or judgment.

The architects who wrote the criteria devised, among other things, a survey method to identify and analyze the visual characteristics of the built environment visible from the public street. Each building and street in the village was observed and recorded by a team of volunteers, using a survey sheet that included thirty-nine elements of architectural character, grouped into three classifications, the building, the site, and the street. Subgroups in the classifications noted those elements that are major (with a primary influence on the visual environment); significant (helping to determine total character in a strong way); and minor (easily altered). This information was then translated into street analysis forms, using percentage figures to describe the degree of similarity and/or differences in each area.

In addition, more than two hundred old photographs of the village were studied. From them and from an analysis of the survey forms and existing buildings of various periods, it became possible to determine the visual character of Hudson and its buildings in each half-century of its history. It had long been recognized that those elements which gave Hudson its distinctive character were from the nineteenth and early twentieth centuries. Now, however, it became clear precisely what those elements were and how they differed from those of later developments. The board approaches blueprints and elevations with some conviction about the features that enhance the uniqueness of the village and those that tend to dilute it.

The ninety-six-page Uniform Architectural Criteria document serves as a guide for the Architectural Board. It has been printed and is available at the Public Library and Village offices. It is hoped that builders and architects will take care to familiarize themselves with it before drawing up plans for buildings and developments.

In December of 1974, the entire downtown area around the green and its contiguous streets was accepted by the National Register of Historic Places as a Historic District. The Village Council and the Planning Commission had been working for some time before this on proposed legislation to create historic-district zoning protection for the area; they viewed the Historic District as a zoning "overlay," all other zoning remaining in effect but with special restrictions superimposed on the Historic District.

This policy was codified in an ordinance passed in March of 1975. The same ordinance reconstitutes the Architectural Board into the Architectural and Historic Board of Review, with a subcommittee of three members to have special care of matters concerning the Historic District. Structures may be built or altered within the District only after the board issues a special certificate of appropriateness and a regular building permit is issued. In practice, the sub-committee reviews the application first and recommends action to the board as a whole. If the application is acceptable, a letter is sent to the applicant, outlining the features that make it appropriate to the district, with a copy to the building inspector, who issues a permit.

The law reads that, if the board recommends that the certificate not be issued, it will "advise the applicant of any changes which would secure the approval of the Board, and withhold denial . . . for a period of not to exceed 30 days, in order that the applicant may adopt such proposed changes." The subcommittee, however, is often able to suggest changes and work out compromises with the applicant before the final plans are reviewed by the board.

The appeal procedure provides for a public hearing, with the Board of Zoning Appeals still the final arbiter. Failure to comply with the decision, after all appeal procedures, results in a fine of from ten dollars to five hundred dollars for each offense. All other procedures and duties of the Architectural Board remain essentially the same.

The campus of Western Reserve Academy was accepted on the National Register of 1976. The Uniform Architectural Criteria recommend that the Historic District be expanded to include the academy and to contain total area of about 240 acres, more than 60 percent of whose buildings date from the nineteenth century. Boundary lines are drawn along back-lot lines, with street center lines used only when great age differences occur on opposite sides. The proposed district also includes some very important nineteenth-century open spaces. When this area is included in the Historic District zoning, almost the whole of the central village will be protected.

It must be remembered, however, that legislation concerning historic districts, architectural boards—or, for that matter, planning commissions or any other local governmental boards or commissions—is subject to particular challenge in Ohio. There is no enabling legislation in the state for any of these. The Home Rule clause, by which any power not specifically delegated to the state may be assumed by an incorporated municipality, is the basis for all locally established bodies. An architectural board, which is so often in danger of being in an adversary position, is particularly vulnerable to the lawsuits that may result. Recently, the Village of Hudson has been involved in two court cases on behalf of the Architectural Board. Fortunately, both were confined to specifics, so that the constitutionality of the board was not called into question. The score for the village is even: one lost, one won.

The major battles now, however, are centered around efforts to keep the green the center of the commercial and social life of the community. The charter of Hudson Heritage states one of its purposes to be the "maintenance of David Hudson's village green and the Hudson public square as the central feature of the Village and Township." During the past five years, many of their efforts, and those of the government of the village, have been directed toward this purpose. Challenges come largely from proposed shopping complexes that would draw customer traffic away from the stores around the green. Village authority does not extend to the township, which, being unincorporated, has only loose zoning codes dictated by the county. Strip developments, therefore, have grown up on the outskirts of the village, particularly to the south. A shopping plaza went up in Hudson itself in 1962.

Since that time, however, it has been recognized that the spirit of the town depends largely on the health of the Main Street enterprises and on the encouragement of pedestrian traffic around the green. A major department store branch, a discount store, or a large grocery chain has no place in the center of the village. It is hoped, rather, that the core of the town will continue to develop into a type of nineteenth-century, open-air, regional shopping center of specialty stores, with ample but inconspicuous parking and convenient, pleasant pedestrian access throughout the

entire area. To that end, it is clear that all further commercial development must be centered around the green and that an integrated plan
must be developed. Attention, therefore, has been focused on two
important undeveloped areas: the so-called Triangle and the south end
of the green.

A seven-acre triangular piece of land lies across from the shopping
plaza, separated from the green by a railroad embankment and overpass.
It was once part of the Kleinman development, and has been platted for
many years for eighty two-family dwellings. Several years ago, its present
owner, a local developer, put forth plans for a shopping center and hotel
on the site. The plans, dependent on a zoning change, required action by
the planning commission, including a public hearing. Feeling that the
shopping center would draw customer traffic away from the green,
Hudson Heritage joined with several homeowners' associations to
oppose the zoning change. A position was circulated. Letters were written
to the Planning Commission by various civic groups. A telephone
campaign was mounted to swell the audience at the public meeting. As a
result, several hundred people attended the hearing, most speaking in
opposition to the zoning change. The final decision of the commission
was to deny the change.

Recently, the same developer has requested rezoning of the site for
single-family condominiums. In this case, his architect studied the new
Uniform Architectural Criteria and met with the Architectural Board to
discuss the general concept. The plan resulting will give the town
approximately fifty much-needed smaller family units, arranged in a
loose scheme that echoes the scale of the nineteenth-century streets in
the village center. The building style is largely contemporary, but with the
deep roof overhangs and the simple but ample framing of window and
door openings characteristic of nineteenth-century Western Reserve
buildings. Units will be loosely arranged for the greatest possible variety in
massing. Parking will be concealed in an interior core, and pedestrian
access and scale emphasized from the public streets. Construction has
not as yet begun, but there is great optimism that the efforts to oppose
another shopping complex away from the green and the months of work
leading to the Uniform Architectural Criteria have at last resulted in the
best possible plan for the Triangle, both in use and visual impact.

Moreover, prospects that future commercial development will, indeed,
be clustered around the south part of the green have brightened since the
passage of a two-and-a-half million-dollar bond issue, in 1976, to finance
the so-called Green Plan.

The plan's roots go back to the local government's pressing need for more space. The ninety-nine-year-old town hall faces the green. Intended to house all governmental facilities for both village and township, the town hall presently is used for the town police forces, the township offices, and a public auditorium. The village has also had to rent space above several of the Main Street stores. One of the pamphlets that was part of the promotional campaign mounted to pass the Green Plan bond issue explains that the village and township, acting jointly, had an opportunity to retain the town green as the political, commercial, and social center of Hudson.

One important element is a meat-cleaver-shaped piece of land extending southeast from the green and including a railroad right of way that also crossed the green's two southern squares. The right of way was granted to the Cleveland and Pittsburgh Railroad in the 1840s, and the adjacent land has never been fully utilized. It is presently vacant and privately owned. The Green Plan provides for the "restoration" of the two squares as green spaces by the removal of the fire station from one and a log cabin used as Boy Scout headquarters from the other. It is hoped that, by freeing and beautifying the public areas and by positive encouragement, the owners of the land around the southern squares of the green will wish to develop them for the type of small retail enterprises for which Hudson is becoming known.

The fire and police departments will be joined in a new Safety Building on one portion of the former railroad land, and an empty warehouse building nearby will be converted to a community center. A site facing the southeast green will be reserved for a possible future town hall. On adjacent land acquired from private sources, Brandywine Creek will be dammed to provide a scenic lake, which engineers have recommended for purposes of flood control.

Meanwhile, with the two police departments moved, the old town hall will be renovated and restored to its original use for governmental offices and meeting rooms. The village council and the township trustees will once again meet in the second-floor auditorium, with its abundant Victorian moldings and its pressed-metal ceiling. The village manager, the Architectural Board, the planning commission, the zoning boards, the Park Board, and the tree commissioner will all be headquartered there once again.

All of this, of course, costs money, and in June of 1976 four bond issues were offered to the voters to finance the plan. It is regarded by many as something of a miracle that the issues passed so decisively. Certainly the passage was due to the work of a dedicated group that left nothing to chance.

As soon as the concept was completed, a topographical scale model of the center of town was constructed, showing the proposed changes. Volunteers drew rough sketches and ground plans for each house in the area, so that any voter could orient himself by recognizing his own home. A partner in a Cleveland design firm, living in the township, was enlisted to help in the selling of the dream, and his professional expertise was essential to the final result.

Slides were taken of the model of the village as it presently stood and then, through successive stages, of the village as it would be if the Green Plan were realized. The model was put on display in a store window and later at the public library. The slides were used for a presentation with simultaneous audio tape, which was professional, persuasive, and moving. It was shown whenever possible at all public meetings.

An ad hoc Citizens Green Committee obtained hostesses in each block who were willing to invite their neighbors in to have coffee and dessert and see the presentation. Importantly, even when only three or four voters were to appear at these neighborhood meetings, some knowledgeable official or member of the Citizens Green Committee was there to answer questions. Four handouts were prepared, including one pictorial pamphlet. Volunteers were stationed at each polling place on Election Day, handing out reminders and offering to answer any last-minute questions. The result was that all four bond issues passed by large majorities in both the village and the township.

The bond issues having been passed, the Green Plan is in the implementation stage, proceeding slowly but almost surely. All the while, other challenges constantly arise. How can we persuade the Post Office to remain on the green? Postal officials have indicated their desire for larger facilities and more parking. What can we do to keep this important facility—which serves both a social and a commercial function by the pedestrian traffic it generates—at the town center? What will, indeed, happen to the privately owned land at the south end of the green? Will the owners be willing to develop for small retail businesses rather than for the more secure income of banks and real estate offices? Will the township elect to consolidate with the village and submit its development to the tighter controls offered by an incorporated municipality before the remaining farms and open spaces around the village disappear? How can new residents and short-term transferees be made aware of the delicacy of the balance that allows for the growth of the community but retains the visual character and quality of life for which they moved to Hudson?

All of these concerns are shared by those in the village and township governments and in organizations like the Hudson Heritage Association, which are working to retain the special charm of Hudson: to preserve its early buildings; to insure that anything new in the built environment enhances the visual character for which the town is known; to maintain the green as the social, political, and commercial center of the community; and to preserve and enlarge the open spaces that are so important to the quality of life.

As Edward N. Fitch, first president of Hudson Heritage, remarked at its first annual meeting in 1962, these purposes are conceived as "the fulfilling of a responsibility—not only to the residents of Hudson whose property values and way of life are strongly influenced by the amenities it seeks to preserve, but to the county, state, and nation, whose pioneer heritage is so well exemplified by the Village and Township of Hudson."

Ipswich, Massachusetts
W. C. K.

Ipswich, Massachusetts (population 12,000), is much older than most places described in this book, having been founded in 1633. From the beginning, Ipswich was a very solid settlement, with well-built houses and a population that included distinguished and wealthy persons from elsewhere in Massachusetts. Free public education began in 1642. The early industries were fishing, lumbering, trapping, and shipbuilding, and the town prospered and grew quickly. As early as 1687 it defied the English Governor Edmund Andros over matters of taxation, and, as a result, calls itself the Birthplace of American Independence. The Revolution, to which Ipswich contributed vigorously, nearly ruined the town, and between 1790 and 1820 the population was halved. The economy remained quiet until mid-nineteenth century, when textile mills started up in the area. The replenished population and revival of trade brought about great changes, and many fine old houses from earlier years remained, though in decreasing numbers. It was these houses, in the 1960s, that historically-minded citizens of Ipswich wanted actively to preserve.

The first event to bring out a latent spirit of revolt was the demolition, in 1960, of a three-hundred-year-old house for a road widening. Then, in 1962, the town moved to demolish another old house. Through the initiative of two women, the second house was reconstructed by the Smithsonian Institution at Washington, in the Museum of History and Technology. In the same year, an oil company proposed to replace a famous house of 1707 with a gas station. This brought about creation of the Ipswich Heritage Trust, a preservation organization sponsored by the seventy-two-year-old Ipswich Historical Society. The trust eventually bought off the oil company and sold the house for professional use with a covenant that preserved both its heavy original frame and its exterior. Furthermore, the trust took and exercised options to purchase on two houses that, like the one they were saving, were on Meeting House Green. The houses were sold with covenants that preserved interior detailing as well as the frames and the exteriors. In such cases, the trust purchased the houses outright for resale, as many similar organizations have done in other towns. The trust charter, however, was designed to allow it to purchase, in other instances, not the house itself, but an easement on the rights to remodel it in certain ways. That proved quite useful; an owner who was fond of the historic character of his house could sell the trust the right to attach a preservation agreement to its deed. Thus the owner knew that, when he died, his house would remain as he had left it, for subsequent owners would be legally bound to leave it so.

Such provisions, in the absence of a large amount of money, could save only a few houses, however. The Ipswich Historical Society and other local organizations therefore prevailed on the board of selectmen (town council) to appoint a Historic District Study Committee, as the laws of Massachusetts empowered them to do. Within the historic districts, approval of a special commission would have been necessary for any alterations visible from a public place. The proposals for such districts were rejected four times by the Massachusetts legislature, however, because the districts proposed were regarded as too large; the owners generally feared governmental interference with their property rights; owners of patently commonplace properties would have had to contend with unnecessary red tape; and it was uncertain how property values would be affected, especially for commonplace properties. For the time being, then, the idea for a historic district was shelved.

In 1964, the town formed a historical commission, whose membership coincided with that of the committee that had studied the historic districts. The commission began modestly, with record-keeping and propaganda. In 1905 the first part of a history of Ipswich had been published, giving a house-by-house account of the past; and an architectural survey of the town had been done in the 1950s. The historic and architectural importance of almost every significant house was thus on record for any citizen, including a property owner, who might care about such things. Some owners, over the years, had put historical plaques on their buildings. The commission organized and continued that work until 1969.

Another commission project was the study of "less-than-fee" interests—in other words, the acquisition of some but not all of the rights to a piece of property—as these rights existed in other places and as they might exist under Massachusetts law. Some communities in the South had experiences that were useful, but the Ipswich commission also studied the use of less-than-fee interests in Great Britain. Such less-than-fee interests were the obvious means for the commission to accomplish its purpose. Unlike the Ipswich Heritage Trust, the commission was a public body, unable to tie up the money that supported it in the outright purchase of property and then to wait for the right buyer. By purchasing a consent, binding on all future owners not to alter a property without the commission's approval, the commission could spend money that it would never get back, but it would avoid the delays and risks of the real estate business.

The legal status of a covenant, or agreement, to preserve portions of a historic building under Massachusetts law was carefully investigated. One interesting question was that of the tax status of a property whose owner had sold to the commission the right to alter it. The commission found that Massachusetts law prohibited assessing the property on the basis of any use that was ruled out by a preservation agreement, though the donation of such an agreement would probably *not* be deductible on the federal income tax returns. The state law happened to encourage preservation agreements, therefore, although the federal law did not.

The securing of sixteen preservation agreements as of 1975 was helped by the U.S. Department of Housing and Urban Development (HUD). HUD, interested in such agreements, signed a contract with the Ipswich Historical Commission for an urban beautification and improvement demonstration project. HUD put up about $21,000, and the Ipswich Heritage Trust donated an equal amount to the historical commission. The success of the project was thus due, in part, to HUD's willingness to subsidize an experiment.

The historical commission saw the preservation agreement as an act of partnership between itself and the property owner who was proud of his property and wanted to see it kept as it was. Both parties were to be satisfied with any such agreement. The standard agreement form finally drawn up was short, clear, and uniform in most respects, though with enough blank spaces to fill in that the particular features of each case could be listed. It stated, first, that in return for a payment to the owner by the commission (one thousand dollars was typical) and in return for technical advice and assistance from the commission, the owner bound himself and future owners not to allow certain alterations (which were specified) to be made to the property without the commission's written approval. The commission was given thirty days to object to any proposed change; after that, the owner was free to make the change. If the commission disapproved, in time, the case could go to a referee appointed by the state historical commission. The referee was given sixty days to notify both parties of his decision. The agreement was to be binding until A.D. 2100 unless otherwise specified.

The agreements worked out with the owners usually protected any part of the building visible from a public way, the structural frame (most Ipswich houses are of wood), and the most interesting decorative objects inside. No attempt was made to tell owners how to paint and paper inside. It is interesting to see that, though owners were *allowed* to make repairs so long as the parts of the building remained the same in appearance, they were not *obligated* to make repairs.

The historical commission's good and careful history of its work, *Something to Preserve,* gives three examples of houses covered by preservation agreements. The first, a house of 1659, had the front and sides, the structural frame, and the wooden interior details that dated from 1659 protected. The rear and any parts of the interior from after 1659 might be altered without commission consent. The importance of the structural frame lay in the fact that, in a house so old, it was exposed inside and was carved with moldings to form part of the decoration. In a house of 1720, the frame was hidden, but the house would have been disrupted if any attempt had been made to change it; it was therefore protected along with most of the visible parts inside and out. In a house built about 1800, a great deal of interior work, much more elaborate than it would have been in older Ipswich houses, was protected. All such agreements were compromises, incidentally. The owners wanted the character of their houses preserved, but there were things about them, usually unimportant, that had to be changed: useless additions to demolish, inconvenient and later-built walls to be torn down, and so on. Furthermore, the owners wanted to be able to add to the houses as they found it convenient, in places where the additions would not spoil the basic appearance.

One tool that the commission found useful was a complete architectural inventory. Using the year 1832 as a cut-off date, the commission inspected every Ipswich building, inside and out. Most property owners co-operated, since they were proud of their buildings. The inspectors made written notes, drawings, and photographs.

As a part of the agreement with HUD, the Ipswich Historical Commission published, in 1975, the book just mentioned—*Something to Preserve,* a history of preservation efforts in the town that concentrated on the demonstration project. The book was intended not only as an official record, but also as an argument for further preservation work, and while it was detailed on all important matters, it was attractively enough presented that the public would be interested in reading it. We have already summarized the main text, but a brief look at the appendixes is interesting, too. They consisted of a "homeowner's common-sense guide to preservation"—what to do and *not* to do in preserving and restoring an old New England house; the state act providing for the establishment of historical commissions and outlining their composition and duties; a state act governing agreements to preserve architecture or areas of landscape from specified types of change; a state act regarding the publication of zoning ordinances and bylaws by towns; a summary of laws regarding historic-preservation restrictions in other New England states; and comments on these laws.

It may be that Ipswich has had unusual advantages. Many New Englanders have a strong sense of their history and are proud of it. The houses the commission and the trust were attempting to preserve were often early Colonial, obviously valuable. And, of course, there happened to be federal money to match that raised by local efforts. It probably helped, too, that the houses were very simple, sturdy ones, easy under most circumstances to maintain and therefore placing no great burden on the owner bound by a preservation agreement.

Old Lyme, Connecticut
W. C. K.

The Historic District of Old Lyme, Connecticut, is close to the village of Essex, whose problems we have already seen; but Old Lyme is different in a number of respects. It is closer to Long Island Sound, though still inland from it, and is bordered not by the Connecticut River itself but by the small, tributary Lieutenant River. Unlike Essex Village, Old Lyme in its early days was not primarily dependent on shipping and shipbuilding, though those trades were important. Livestock breeding, fishing, wood processing, and quarrying were other industries that kept the village prosperous through the middle of the nineteenth century. The original village, the present historic district, was laid out along Lyme Street, a broad street that runs parallel to the Lieutenant River for the better part of a mile. Because of the importance of farming, properties tended to have much broader street frontages than those on the Main Street of Essex, and the early prosperity of the village was such that some houses in Lyme are much more pretentious than their counterparts across the river.

In the late nineteenth century, the economic base of Old Lyme was badly eroded, and many persons moved away. Certain of the houses became boarding schools, while one of the grandest houses in town, that of Florence Griswold, was turned into a boarding house for the artists who, by the turn of the century, had become attracted to the village. The influence of Florence Griswold was such that the wealthy soon discovered Old Lyme for themselves and began to build there or buy up the older houses. In 1907, when the famous Federal-style Congregational Church burned down, the village was prosperous enough to put up a replica. By 1920, Old Lyme was so solidly established as an artistic center that Charles A. Platt, architect of the Freer Gallery in Washington—his specialty was mansions—was commissioned to design a fair-sized art gallery.

Today, the historic district of Old Lyme enjoys visible prosperity and precarious seclusion. Lyme Street, the spine of the historic district, has a definite beginning and end. Its feeder roads serve purely local traffic at the south end, although the northern part, a convenient approach to Interstate 95, gets some fast, disruptive traffic. Tourism and yachting have never been promoted. There are a very few discreet shops in the historic district and two restaurants, established in old houses; otherwise, there is no commerce. Art lovers are attracted to the Florence Griswold house and the art gallery, but neither place is a great tourist attraction. All in all, the historic district is lovely, unspoiled, and a place to be lived in rather than looked at. It contains seventy-one properties, fifty of them with pre-1900 buildings and eight with buildings from before 1800. North of the district is more recent and less interesting development, but beyond that, and to the east, are wooded hills. To the west, between the Lieutenant and the Connecticut rivers, the land is marshy and full of interesting flora and fauna. In the areas to the south, down by the shore, development is decidedly haphazard and often lamentable. The historic district is thus a markedly civilized place caught between the wilderness of the Connecticut valley and the cluttered beach areas of Long Island Sound. Its one jarring feature is I-95, the Connecticut Turnpike, which crosses Lyme Street on an arched, stone-faced overpass.

Early in 1967, some citizens of Old Lyme began to feel that conventional development was threatening the Lyme Street area and began to agitate for historic-district zoning. The Old Lyme Conservation Trust, whose purpose is to acquire and preserve the adjacent marshlands, had been founded in the previous year, and the creation of a historic district was regarded as a complementary measure, an extension to the man-made environment of the protection that the natural environment was beginning to receive.

A telephone campaign, followed by a town meeting, brought the project into the open. Preservationists distributed copies of the National Historic Preservation Act of 1966, and argued that property values would rise in a historic district. The threat imposed by I-95 also stimulated them to apply for admission to the National Register of Historic Places, which would inhibit the spoiling of Lyme Street by any federally funded works. In October 1967 the selectmen (town council) of Old Lyme appointed a Historic District Study Committee to investigate the situation and prepare a report. This report first appeared in June 1970, and a final version, with the documents to date, was published five months later, in December. Under laws dating from 1963, a Connecticut community is empowered to establish a historic district, controlled by a local commission with specified powers, provided that certain conditions are met. Of these conditions, the most important is that the proposed ordinance be approved by the Connecticut Historical Commission, certain town officials, and 75 percent of the property owners in the proposed district.

Although an exhibition of Old Lyme properties as they were in the past and as they were in the late 1960s was important in gaining the necessary citizen approval, and although word-of-mouth propaganda doubtless helped, the major instrument for the legalization of the historic district was the report itself. In its final version of December 1970, it contained the following material: letters of approval from the Connecticut Historical

Commission, the board of selectmen, the zoning commission, and the planning commission; excerpts from the National Historic Preservation Act of 1966 regarding the importance of preservation; a preamble to the report; a statement of the purpose of a historic district; a history of Old Lyme; a brief architectural guide to the proposed district, with nineteen illustrated examples; a map showing every property affected (two regional maps appear elsewhere); an analysis, by period of construction, of seventy-one properties; a map showing, in detail, a second possible historic district; the proposed ordinance, which specified boundaries, the organizational structure of the historic district commission, its powers as defined by the General Statutes of Connecticut, and the effective date; excerpts from the General Statutes of Connecticut; a copy of the general notice of a public meeting on the question; and an amendment to the proposed ordinance. The report, as submitted to the various government bodies, was approved without reservation.

In March 1971, a secret ballot of property owners voted for the historic district by an overwhelming majority; at a subsequent town meeting, the motion for the district was almost unanimously carried. In October 1971, the historic district was placed on the National Register of Historic Places.

Galveston, Texas

Peter Brink, Galveston Historical Foundation

Galveston is an island—some say a large sandbar—a mile off the Texas coast in the Gulf of Mexico, forty-five miles southeast of Houston. Its present-day economy rests mainly on some four million tourists annually (still drawn principally by its thirty miles of beaches and temperate climate), a deep-water port, and a major medical complex. Its population of 70,000 residents reflects the ethnic diversity of a seaport community, and nearly half of this total are blacks and Mexican-Americans. The city is not well off economically, with average per-capita income of $1,344 in 1976 and 21 percent of the population at poverty level.

More remarkable for preservationists, however, are the more than one thousand nineteenth-century residential and commercial structures intact today, constituting one of the finest such concentrations in the nation. Ironic twists of history have both created these structures and allowed them to survive.

In the mid-nineteenth century, Galveston and its deep-water port were already the commercial hub of Texas, with cotton flowing out from much of the Southwest and manufactured goods and immigrants flowing in. Thriving merchants and bankers constructed imposing Victorian commercial buildings near the wharves along a street grandly named the Strand (after London's) and dubbed "the Wall Street of the Southwest." With such prosperity, the wealthiest families built grand mansions along palm-lined boulevards, while thousands of other families constructed substantial frame houses and raised cottages throughout the city.

In 1900 Galveston survived the Great Storm and responded vigorously by building a massive sea wall and raising the grade level of the city seven feet—and then, by the 1920s, the city found commercial growth bypassing it for nearby Houston, with its newly dredged ship channel. Yet it was that very lack of economic growth in the twentieth century that saved Galveston's nineteenth-century areas from large-scale demolition.

Origins of the Historical Foundation

By the 1960s the reprieve for nineteenth-century Galveston was yielding to economic pressures, and arbitrary demolitions and spots of strip development were causing the loss of key structures. Preservation by inaction, rather than by design, was no longer an adequate solution.

Fortunately, however, Galvestonians and others were beginning to recognize what a vast treasure of nineteenth-century structures the island possessed. A major sign of that new appreciation appeared in the 1950s. Until then, the Galveston Historical Society, founded in 1871, had been essentially a literary society. During 1954, however, the 1839 home of Samuel May Williams, a leader of the Republic of Texas, was about to be demolished. Seven spirited and outraged ladies of the Galveston Historical Society stopped that, single-handedly raising the funds to purchase and preserve the property. Equally important, they incorporated the society as the Galveston Historical Foundation and extended its purposes to saving historic structures.

Then, in 1966, the handsome book *The Galveston That Was,* by Houston architect Howard Barnstone, with photographs by Henri Cartier-Bresson and Ezra Stoller, was published. The book brought to thousands of readers the unique beauty of historic Galveston, although the tone of the book was sad, since it was intended to show us these good and beautiful things before the forces of the world destroyed them forever.

Some strong souls, however, refused to accept the normal way of things, and in the next several years they braved a generally apathetic community to save endangered parts of historic Galveston.

"Bishop's Palace," the Walter Gresham residence in Galveston, Texas, was designed by Nicholas Clayton and built in 1886. It has been selected as one of the one hundred outstanding examples of American architecture and is open for tours. The sign in the foreground identifies it for visitors. — Galveston Historical Foundation. Photograph by Sue King

Thus, by 1969, the historical foundation, with a grant from the Galveston-based Moody Foundation, was carrying out a survey-and-planning project so that two locally zoned historical districts could be established: a forty-block residential area (the East End) and a ten-block commercial area (the Strand). In 1971 the city council approved the East End Historical District, but denied the Strand proposal because of strong opposition from existing Strand owners.

In spite of this mixed success, the Strand was nevertheless listed as a historic district on the National Register through the efforts of the Texas Historical Commission. Simultaneously, the Junior League of Galveston took the pioneering steps of purchasing and restoring two key Strand buildings, one for its own offices and the other for a cultural center.

At the same time, in that tumultuous period, the historical foundation was leading a community effort to prevent demolition of one of the city's grand mansions, the 1859 Ashton Villa, an Italianate structure located on a main boulevard. After years of struggle and with the help of acquisition grants by the Moody Foundation and the U.S. Department of Housing and Urban Development, Ashton Villa was finally saved, with title in the city and restoration/administrative responsibility in the historical foundation.

Finally, the Kempner Fund of Galveston quietly initiated, with the historical foundation, a program under which some six houses in the East End District were restored and sold to young professionals, and the historical foundation saved from destruction St. Joseph's Church, a small frame structure built in 1859.

The Present Effort

In 1973 the efforts of preservationists were elevated to a new level of intensity. The major impetus was realization that a much more comprehensive approach was needed to save and revitalize the Strand. While, in addition to the Junior League's work, the Galveston County Cultural Arts Council had established an active arts center in the Strand, a strategy was needed to attract a sufficient number of economically viable uses to assure preservation of buildings throughout the district. Thus, leaders of the Galveston Historical Foundation and Arts Council initiated the idea of a revolving fund, and the Arts Council obtained a seed-money grant from the National Endowment for the Arts to bring in Lee Adler of Savannah and Arthur Ziegler of Pittsburgh to advise on the importance and methodology of such a program. As a result of these efforts, the Moody Foundation granted $200,000 and the Kempner Fund $15,000 to the historical foundation to establish the Strand Revolving Fund.

By the spring of 1973, an executive director (myself, Peter Brink) had been recruited by the historical foundation to organize and operate the revolving fund. With many Strand buildings deteriorated, vacant, or under-used, the goal of the fund was to achieve the preservation, appropriate rehabilitation, and active use of available buildings. The Strand was to be revitalized with apartments, retail shops, restaurants, exhibit areas, and offices, while retaining existing wholesale businesses. What was wanted was neither a staged tourist set nor a museum, but an area frequented by both Galvestonians and visitors because of its vitality, variety of uses and activities, close ties to other key areas of the city, and the particular beauty of its nineteenth-century buildings. Of special importance was strong participation by the arts and the artists and close linkages with the port area, where vessels, visible a block away, lend a unique drama to the Strand.

Adaptive use works well in Galveston, Texas. The city's First National Bank, seen here on the corner of the Strand and Kempner, dates from 1877 and was the first federally chartered bank in Texas. Today, it serves as the Galveston Arts Center on the Strand, its handsome lobby a gallery. To the right of it is the Trueheart-Adriance Building, designed by Nicholas Clayton and dating from 1882. Recently restored by the Junior League of Galveston, it now houses their successful sandwich shop and restaurant. At far right is the Kauffman-Runge Building (1882), now housing the Stewart Title Company, which has received recognition from the National Trust for Historic Preservation for its recent restoration of the building's exterior. — Galveston Historical Foundation. Photograph by Sue King

The heart of these efforts was the revolving fund, with which Strand buildings were to be purchased and then re-sold for active use, with preservation deed restriction and restoration/development requirements. Work thus began on the multiple tasks necessary to make the fund work and to accomplish the goals of the Strand effort. These tasks included reorganization of the historical foundation and broadening community participation; purchasing of initial properties; working out of deed restrictions and contractual undertakings for purchasers; arrangement of special long-term financing with local lenders for rehabilitation of the properties; pricing and improvements; and work on fire prevention, traffic, parking, and security. In addition, an over-all Strand plan was completed, by 1975, with the Philadelphia architects Venturi and Rauch, through funding from the National Endowment for the Arts, while major public events such as "Dickens's Evening on The Strand" each December and, in past years, "Festival on the Strand" drew thousands of visitors to see the Strand's potential.[1]

Galveston's Joseph Ricke Cottage, built in 1856–1857, in the simple, Classical Revival style, is reminiscent of the pioneer cottages of the German settlers of central Texas. — Galveston Historical Foundation. Photograph by Vaden Smith

GALVESTON 19TH CENTURY HOMES

The Galveston Historical Foundation puts its architectural resources to work for their own good: a collage of handsome buildings appears here on the title page of a book in which they figure. —Galveston Historical Foundation

In looking back over our five years of work with the revolving fund, one sees that important things have been accomplished:

- More than $4 million in private investments have been attracted for rehabilitation of Strand buildings and active uses in them.
- Nineteen Strand buildings have been extensively rehabilitated and are protected by deed restrictions.
- People are frequenting the once-deserted Strand and patronizing some seventeen restaurants, shops, and exhibit areas.
- Twenty apartments have been completed in upper floors of the buildings, with their residents forming the nucleus of a Strand neighborhood.
- Capital improvements, such as period lighting, a *trompe l'oeil* (real-looking) architectural mural, a street park, and a system of pictorial signs for walking tours have been completed.
- Small boats have been allowed to remain at Pier 19, as a result of public referendum, retaining for the public this maritime historical area adjacent to the Strand.
- The 250,000-square-foot Art Deco Santa Fe Building and Terminal, once slated for demolition, has been bought by the Moody Foundation, and its renovation for offices and a major railroad museum has begun.
- The city has obtained a $3 million HUD grant to construct a cruise ship terminal and parking structure on vacant land in the Strand District and to assist the Arts Council in rehabilitating the 1894 Grand Opera House in the downtown area as a major performing arts center.
- The Strand District has been recognized as a National Historic Landmark [one of about 1,000 on a special National Register], as has the East End Historical District.
- The Historical Foundation has received (in 1978) a second revolving-fund grant of $150,000 from the Moody Foundation to extend its efforts to the next street adjacent to the Strand.

At the same time, one must list several frustrations or failures:

- The pace of the effort, both in rehabilitation and drawing of people, has been slower than expected; everything takes longer than one expects, from buying a building to selling a building to completion of rehabilitation, and so on, and there are always *more* essential things that need to be done after one has accomplished what appeared to be *the* essential achievement. Indeed, it will probably be two more years before the Santa Fe development and cruise-ship terminal are completed.

- The historical foundation has not been about to accomplish revitalization of the Strand without losing a substantial part of the capital of its initial revolving fund (one supporter now calls it "the evaporating fund"). The *capital* portion of our 1973 grants totalled $165,000, of which we have $25,000 remaining as of 1977. In many ways, the hope of accomplishing so much preservation and rehab work with no capital cost was a very misleading one; one should view this "loss" as a community investment that has levered a tremendous amount of private investment.

- Although the historical foundation has done a great deal with deed restrictions, it has refrained from again seeking a locally zoned historical district for the Strand; that strategy has won the co-operation of most existing owners, but resulted in the loss of an 1866 building after a divisive legal battle with a local bank.

- The historical foundation has still not fully succeeded in placing retail uses among existing wholesalers; a major block of wholesalers separates the retail concentrations, causing many visitors to miss one or other of the concentrations.

Aside from the Strand program, the historical foundation has grown to be a major community organization. It had, in 1977, a paid membership of 2,100, with an effective newsletter and good media coverage to keep the community informed of its work. It completed restoration of Ashton Villa in 1974, and by 1977 drew 40,000 persons annually on quality tours of the mansion, as well as users to its Visitor's Center and its large ballroom for receptions and special events. It has done an exhaustive restoration study of the Samuel May Williams House and will soon restore and open it for public tours and other uses. It has undertaken restoration of an 1877 square-rigged sailing vessel, the *Elissa,* which will be a major maritime exhibit for the Gulf Coast. Its programs division has developed a superb annual homes tour, group heritage tours throughout the year, the magical "Dickens's Evening on The Strand" drawing some 40,000 visitors, and broad community educational and research programs. The foundation, with government funding, has completed a comprehensive historical survey of Galveston and an extensive study of neighborhood preservation and historical districts to assist the city's administration of the East End and Silk Stocking districts.

Nevertheless, the great number of historic structures and neighborhoods existing in Galveston is rather overwhelming. The resources and

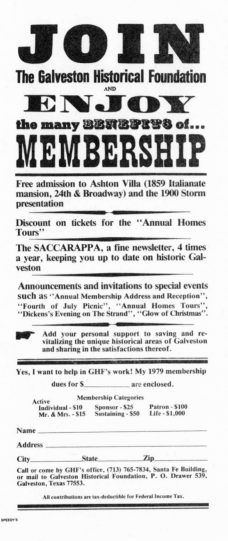

Recruiting poster devised by the Galveston Historical Foundation stresses benefits of membership in the foundation and includes a membership application.—Galveston Historical Foundation

supporters of preservation are often stretched so thin handling the on-going efforts mentioned above, as well as unavoidable emergencies such as impending demolitions, that two related areas of great importance have not been addressed adequately. One is the complex and delicate challenge of assisting residential neighborhoods not now protected by historic-district zoning in protecting and rehabilitating structures and in forming neighborhood associations. The other is the involvement of blacks and Mexican-Americans more fully in the work of the foundation, especially in neighborhood preservation work. As existing efforts attain success, resources are slowly being shifted to meet these other needs, and a planning effort is now under way so that these key needs are not overlooked.

In looking beyond the specific achievements of the historical foundation to the methods that have enabled it to succeed in many cases, several things stand out:

First, the foundation is able to combine outstanding volunteer leadership with a paid staff. Giving volunteer leaders major areas of responsibility, with necessary back-up and help from staff, has enabled major

Visitors tour the Strand in Galveston, Texas, as part of the Galveston Historical Foundation's Heritage Tours program. These popular all-day excursions to Galveston historical sites include stops at private historic homes not open to the public. — Galveston Historical Foundation. Photograph by Sue King

undertakings such as programs, the *Elissa,* Ashton Villa, and the Williams House to succeed.

Second, by carrying out its priorities in a vigorous and competent manner, the historical foundation has earned solid credibility in the community, enabling it to influence a broader area of preservation concerns. Slowly, the foundation is becoming a catalyst, but only after proving its worth to the community as a doer.

Third, a strong effort is continually being made to gain a broad base of members and supporters so that the organization, while still supported by wealthy and influential persons, is open to all and is rooted deeply in the community.

Fourth, strong community support is being combined with effective fund-raising from both private foundations and donors and from a range of government programs; three of the most valuable government programs have been the National Endowment for the Arts for planning work, Interior Department Grants-in-Aid from the Texas Historical Commission for acquisition and development of properties, the CETA job-training positions through the city and county (the historical foundation in 1977 had fifteen CETA staff positions, ranging from photographer to secretary to gardener, which have greatly multiplied its effectiveness).

Fifth, the activity of a communitywide preservation organization like the historical foundation spurs and complements the achievements of other organizations and individuals; thus in Galveston we have seen the emergence of strong neighborhood associations in the historical districts, a multiplicity of individual restorations undertaken, and churches and other organizations caring for their own irreplaceable structures.

Underlying all of these methods and achievements of the Galveston Historical Foundation is, of course, the dedication and ability of the leadership and participants in the organization. Only a deep belief in the value of historic preservation for Galveston and warm satisfaction from each small triumph overcome the difficulty of carrying out community preservation work day after day and year after year. For those of such a bent, however, it is a most enriching experience.

1. For a detailed explanation of the operation of the Strand Revolving Fund, please see "Commercial Area Revolving Funds for Preservation," an information paper published by the National Trust for Historic Preservation.

Murfreesboro, Tennessee

James K. Huhta, Director of Historic Preservation
Middle Tennessee State University, Murfreesboro

Murfreesboro, Tennessee, county seat of Rutherford County, lies thirty-five miles southeast of Nashville in the geographic center of the state. A growing community of almost forty thousand, Murfreesboro was settled originally as Cannonsburgh and traces its origins to 1811. For a time Murfreesborough, as it was originally spelled, served as the capital of Tennessee. By the time of the Civil War, the area reflected the economic and political powers of its large cotton-growing economy: its new county courthouse, then recently completed, and a bustling commercial area around the public square dominated the townscape. Visible from the roof of the courthouse were dozens of townhouse properties, the proud architectural treasures of plantation owners whose fields stretched to the horizon in every direction.

During the Civil War, Murfreesboro, so near Tennessee's capital, became a prime military objective and was for a time Confederate General Braxton Bragg's headquarters. At the Battle of Stones River, fought just outside Murfreesboro, Union forces under General William Rosecrans routed Confederate troops and occupied the town, confirming Union control of the Mid-South in 1863 with the building of Fortress Rosecrans, the largest system of earthwork fortifications ever constructed in the United States.

In the century that followed, Murfreesboro entered a period of moderate growth not to be broken until the "Sunbelt" migration of northern industry after World War II began a cycle of rapid industrial and commercial growth. By 1950, the fine residential areas to the south and southwest of the city's public square had been replaced by "strip blight." Ironically, a serious flood in the late 1940s probably prevented the strip-blight phenomenon from destroying the outstanding mid- to late-nineteenth-century neighborhoods east and northwest of the public square. The flood prompted an urban renewal project resulting in construction of a highway bypass to the west of the square. The new road, Broad Street, served to remove the pressure for commercial redevelopment that had threatened the remaining early residential neighborhoods. Today Broad Street is an ugly example of strip blight at its worst, but its saving grace is the role it played in preserving several early residential neighborhoods.

The "Broad Street incident" probably alerted community leaders for more careful consideration of the need to conserve the best of the community's early building stock while using urban renewal to remove genuine blight.

In 1959, when land was sought for construction of much-needed public housing for economically deprived persons, the last remaining acreage of the once-extensive Oaklands plantation, site of Oaklands mansion, was selected as a likely possibility. Public officials responded affirmatively; but a group of determined women in the community organized the Oaklands Association and requested that the mansion be saved. Recognizing its significance as a showcase of Federal to Italianate architectural evolution between the 1810s and the Civil War, the group proposed to develop it into a historic house museum, portraying both architectural evolution and antebellum Southern life. Responding to community feeling, the city deeded the house and a protective land buffer to the newly formed Oaklands Association. The property was thus saved and, after extensive restoration and furnishing, is open to the public today. Over the years, the bulk of the funds needed for continued

Murfreesboro does not lack for grand architecture and has lost less of it than many communities. One of the reasons is an increased public awareness created by preservation projects.

development of the Oaklands site have come from fund-raising efforts such as a Christmas open house, an Old South Ball, and an annual antique show. Other funds have come from the state historic preservation office, either as state monies or as matching grants from the U.S. Department of the Interior.

One major immediate effect of the effort to save the Oaklands mansion was seen in the public debate over providing county offices with additional space. One option included destruction of the antebellum courthouse, while another possibility looked to resolve the space needs through an addition to the existing building. Public outcry against demolition of the old courthouse not only saved the building, but was also responsible for the approval of plans for construction of two new wings—of such careful and sensitive design that they appear to be of the same antiquity as the original building.

The Stones River National Battlefield, just north of Murfreesboro and adjacent to the National Cemetery, was established in the 1920s on the site of the Civil War battlefield and was a dormant resource into the 1970s. Except for a brief flurry of activity during the Civil War Centennial, marked here with the construction of a visitors' center, the national battlefield had stood remote from the community. A new superintendent arriving on the scene initiated efforts to make the site an important resource for the community, as well as for the outside visitor. Very rarely is that kind of co-operation and interest demonstrated, but an alliance between such a facility and community preservation interests can be most helpful to all concerned.

Early in the 1970s, the state historic preservation office sponsored a brief survey of the community, resulting in several properties being placed on the National Register of Historic Places. This recognition of the Rutherford County Courthouse, Fortress Rosecrans, Oaklands, and several architecturally and/or historically significant residential prop-erties opened a new chapter in this community's preservation history. At about the same time—1973—several other elements coalesced to play significant community roles in the future.

The Murfreesboro Architecture and Zoning Society (MAZS) was founded in reaction to an ill-conceived proposal by traffic planners for widening East Main Street, "to facilitate the flow of traffic." East Main Street is the community's finest residential corridor—a show-case of 150 years of architectural evolution in Murfreesboro, and it is lined with hundreds of centuries-old trees that the aborted plan could have destroyed.

Begun originally by East Main residents, MAZS grew rapidly in membership and programs when its founders began monitoring major community zoning and development matters, promoting public interest in and awareness of the community's existing architecture, and stressing better standards for new architecture. A program of MAZS architectural awards was initiated in 1974. Each year since, properties nominated for architectural merit (old, new, commercial, residential, and public) and/or excellence in landscaping are reviewed by a competent outside authority. An annual awards banquet is held for members, nominees, public officials, and the community at large. Finalists, selected by the outside judge, each year receive a beautiful certificate and are eligible to display a large metal plaque on their property. More than one hundred awards have been made, to date. The program has succeeded in increasing public appreciation, sympathy, and understanding of the need to preserve the best of our older buildings, while setting higher standards of aesthetic quality for new construction. The landscaping program also has succeeded in raising standards for community beautification.

In a major public confrontation, MAZS sought to flex the muscle of its growing membership base (then more than three hundred, now more

Murfreesboro's Opera House is a good example of adaptive utilization to maintain a building in continuous use. Originally an opera house, a theater, later a retail store, this building is being modernized in the interior to provide up-to-date office space, while the outside is undergoing restoration of the original theater facade.

The vernacular housing of Murfreesboro, like that of many small towns, is relatively intact and is a major resource. There is an increased awareness of the value of keeping such buildings preserved in much their original state.

than five hundred), when the community's oldest financial institution acquired, as the site for much-needed expansion, the landmark James K. Polk Hotel (recently closed, a victim to newly constructed motels outside the city). MAZS had worked for more than a year to seek alternative uses for this 1920s property as a county office building or as a senior citizens' housing center. Federal tax incentive and senior citizen housing programs, which would come into being several years later, were not available at that time to make such alternative uses feasible. Again, a typical American preservation scenario began to develop: a community preservation group versus a powerful financial institution. The confrontation never materialized, however. Quiet negotiations between interested citizens, MAZS officers, and bank officials concluded in a gentlemen's agreement to apply an important preservation tool: when no economically feasible alternative exists to protect a private property from demolition, then the building to be constructed in its place should exceed in aesthetic quality that which is replaced. The bank's public announcement of a distinguished new building reflecting the nineteenth-century architectural heritage of the community was greeted warmly by MAZS and the general public. The sincerity supporting the project was reflected in a heavily attended public ceremony when, upon completion of the new building, the Murfreesboro Bank and Trust Company was presented a special award of appreciation by MAZS for the bank's commitment to downtown revitalization through the promotion of good new architectural standards. In this respect, preservation looks not only at the matter of protecting the existing building stock, but urges also new construction that will enhance the quality of a community's built environment.

Contributing also to the quickening of community interest in historic preservation was the establishment, at Middle Tennessee State University, in Murfreesboro, of the first undergraduate program in historic preservation in the United States. That program, begun in 1973, and its graduate equivalent, begun in 1974, brought hundreds of young people from across the United States to study at the university and to work actively, from books to bricks, in the community on major preservation needs. Not only did the community benefit from this infusion of determined young people, but the "real-world" experience of such public service community involvement served the students well as they entered dozens of historic preservation positions outside of Tennessee. By 1979, the MTSU historic preservation program was assisting communities in more than twenty midwestern, mid-southern, and southeastern states to develop preservation components for their community development plans.

A major public awareness conference, funded by the Tennessee Committee for the Humanities through the financial assistance of the National Endowment for the Humanities, was held in 1975 to focus attention on problems common to preservation in metropolitan areas and older suburban communities. Entitled "Small Town–Big Town: Our Town," the conference was jointly sponsored by MAZS, the MTSU Historic Preservation Program, the Metropolitan Historical Commission of Nashville, and Historic Nashville, Inc. The two-day conference brought together hundreds of interested citizens to hear a number of nationally recognized preservation leaders, including Arthur Ziegler of Pittsburgh, and locally involved preservationists. Much of the recent public awareness of and support for historic preservation in both Murfreesboro and Nashville would trace their origins in part to the widespread publicity received by the conference.

With the coming of the American Revolution Bicentennial, a broad base of interest in the cultural heritage of the community would be tapped. Through the efforts of the "Horizons '76" program of the local bicentennial effort, major beginnings were made in a number of areas.

This bank, in visual proximity to the courthouse and the public square in Murfreesboro, worked closely with community preservationist groups when it planned and put up its new building. The result is an aesthetic mix of old and new. In this instance, the effort was successfully made to design a modern building that blends with the existing environment, rather than to imitate past styles.

The largest project and the one nearest completion today — the Cannonsburgh living history project—began in 1974 as a public works program to train unemployed persons in new skills. Other funds were provided by the U.S. Department of Commerce, U.S. Department of Labor, and the U.S. Department of Housing and Urban Development.

More than a thousand other local citizens, in addition to the unemployed trainees, volunteered for work on Cannonsburgh. The development was undertaken to get rid of ramshackle corrugated-steel warehouses in a two-city-block area and replace them with some means of promoting public interest in and awareness of historic preservation in Murfreesboro. Within two years, a fifteen-building, open-air, living-history project had been launched. Today, once-commonplace resources from the immediate vicinity have been assembled at Cannonsburgh, depicting the century of development from 1815 to about 1915. The project now includes a blacksmith shop, a gristmill, a schoolhouse, a church building, a town hall, log cabin, log house, and a general store. An early cotton gin built there originally and its adjacent warehouse were saved. Although not completed at the time of this writing, the project has been open to the public for three seasons and has attracted more than 175,000 visitors. More important, the project has served vitally to promote public support of and public confidence in historic preservation as an aid to community development. The local Chamber of Commerce did not have to be persuaded to relocate its offices into an adaptively restored log house adjacent to the Cannonsburgh site. Soon afterward, the chamber established a separate committee or council to advise the Chamber of Commerce Board of Directors on matters related to "historic preservation, historic zoning, and downtown revitalization." There were also many important economic spin-offs that benefited the community financially: tourism-related dollar volume had, in four years, increased from the approximately $3 million invested in the local economy in 1974 to more than $26 million in 1978. An effective promotional effort to build public support for historic preservation must always assess the potential economic impact that community preservation projects can have on tourism development.

At about the same time, work also was started on the restoration of the antebellum Rutherford County Courthouse, through funding by the county government and the U.S. Department of Interior preservation monies. Progress began on a downtown revitalization effort, stimulated by the courthouse project and the efforts of several private-property owners to upgrade their holdings. A grant from the U.S. Department of the Interior was matched by the city of Murfreesboro to finance

Two of the buildings in Cannonsburgh are shown here—a blacksmith shop and the original building that served as a cotton warehouse, which now contains a museum portraying the community's early development. The Cannonsburgh project has served to focus community interest on the city's architectural heritage and to make people more aware of the need for preservation.

The Rutherford County courthouse is still the center of much activity, and the square around it is alive and healthy. The restoration work on the cupola is jointly funded by county monies matching a grant from the U.S. Department of the Interior. Other work on the courthouse interior is in progress. Although the inner space will be adapted to modern uses, much of its original flavor will be kept by sensitive use of materials and methods. The exterior will be kept in its original state.

documentary research and archeological explorations that laid the basis for the restoration of Fortress Rosecrans, the three-hundred-acre site of which had been acquired by the city of Murfreesboro with the assistance of federal Bureau of Outdoor Recreation funds. A beautiful setting in Old Fort Park became the home of Rosecrans Centre, an outdoor amphitheater developed with federal community development grant monies. The center promotes the heritage of the area through outdoor musicals and dramatic productions.

Finally, the Old City Cemetery, closed in the 1870s, was completely restored with U.S. Department of Housing and Urban Development funds, as a means of refurbishing this major "green space" area in the center-city.

In 1979, the principal historic preservation issue before the citizens of Murfreesboro was that of historic district zoning. An *ad hoc* historic zoning commission of five citizens had been appointed in 1978 by the mayor and the city council to study the feasibility of historic zoning for the community. Early in 1979, major studies, prepared as a public service by the Middle Tennessee State University Historic Preservation Program and with an estimated value of $25,000, were made public. The studies reviewed three areas for possible historic zoning: the public square commercial area, the East Main Street area, and a racially and economically mixed neighborhood near Oaklands. These three areas are representative of almost fifty city blocks containing remarkably intact residential and commercial resources that span the community's 175-year history. As of this writing, the commission has endorsed a proposed historic zoning ordinance and sent the matter to the City Planning Commission for further review. Ultimately, the ordinance will reach the city council, which will hold public hearings to measure citizen support of historic zoning. The various new federal tax incentives for the preservation of income-producing properties have brought many in the commercial sector forward as proponents of historic zoning. The Murfreesboro Chamber of Commerce and MAZS are also expected to support the concept.

Other organizations expected to ally themselves in support of historic zoning include the local chapter of the League of Women Voters and the Murfreesboro Beautification Commission. The League of Women Voters has played an important role for more than ten years in its careful studies and public forums on matters related to community planning, zoning, and development. In recent years, the Murfreesboro Beautification Commission, appointed by the mayor, has evolved into an indirect

Much of the distinctive brick work on Murfreesboro's public square was covered over with the "improvements" that came in the 1950s. Part of the rich variety in the original decorative treatment of building facades can be seen in the two quite different but wholly compatible restored buildings in the foreground.

This scene from Murfreesboro's public square shows both preservation and restoration at work. The store on the left still functions well in its original form, with its charming signs. The white building to the right retains the general character of the original, older structure, but it has been changed enough to adapt the space inside to modern use.

preservation vehicle through its active programs in support of community cleanliness, beauty, and general environmental awareness.

The creation of Tennessee's first regional preservation specialist, to serve the thirteen-county regional planning and economic development district in which Murfreesboro is located, has already proven to be a godsend for local preservation, as progress had placed increased demands for services on an already overloaded state historic preservation office. This regional officer provides professional preservation assistance to individuals, company officials, and organizations needing such aid. The Tennessee regional-preservation planner program was implemented in 1977, after careful study of a similar, long-established program in South Carolina and a recently created program of that kind in Georgia.

An element of the "Murfreesboro Story" deserving special comment is the role played by the two local newspapers, the *Daily News Journal* and the *Press*, and two neighboring newspapers, the *Nashville Tennessean* and the *Nashville Banner*, in weekly area editions, publicizing and supporting community-based historic preservation projects.

It is important to note here that the greatest financial contributions for the projects discussed have come through the identification and analysis

Good adaptive use of its interior space has helped to restore and maintain the stately formality and disciplined style of the Clark House, now providing distinctive space for professional offices in Murfreesboro.

of many federal programs, those sponsored by the U.S. departments of Commerce, Interior, Labor, and Housing and Urban Development, especially. An account of the programs used in Murfreesboro is not particularly useful, here, given continuing changes in the federal program. What *is* of consequence is the importance of obtaining early information on proposed undertakings by the federal government. Any individual or group interested in careful monitoring of changing federal financial aid programs is advised to subscribe to the *Catalog of Federal Domestic Assistance* published annually (with periodic revisions) by the U.S. Government Printing Office. The current annual subscription price of eighteen dollars includes the catalogues and — normally — two updates, each almost two thousand pages in length. Even more careful monitoring is possible through study of the *Federal Register*, published every working day of the year, for a total of more than seventy thousand

Four views of unusual preservation opportunities in Murfreesboro: upper left is a nearly unchanged Art Deco storefront. Upper right shows that old painted signs can be both historical evidence and aesthetically pleasing. Lower left is distinctly small-town: the fence lines in an alley are much the same as they were decades ago. Lower right is a sign of past times and present, done in the dying art of neon.

pages and available from the U.S. Government Printing office for forty-nine dollars.

What does the future hold for historic preservation in Murfreesboro? The most immediate principal activities will probably concern historic district zoning, neighborhood conservation, and downtown revitalization through use of tax incentives. Whether the future for historic preservation in Murfreesboro will be bright or not is not so material as is the fact that the community and its leaders are aware of the important role that a sound historic preservation component can play in improving the quality of life and the quality of the built environment, promoting balanced economic development, and creating a sense of pride, involvement, time, and place.

Appendix 1:
General Advice

There are several things that anyone seriously interested in historic preservation should do. Among them are the following:

Join the National Trust for Historic Preservation, 1785 Massachusetts Avenue, N.W., Washington, D.C. 20036. The National Trust is a preservation organization chartered by Congress. It publishes a quarterly, *Historic Preservation,* discussing specific projects and problems, and a monthly paper, *Preservation News,* with information about what is happening currently, including new laws and court decisions. It also has literature intended to give information and advice on specific problems. Through the Trust it may be possible to get professional advice, or loans, or grants of money. Write the Trust, join (personal membership, $10, association membership, $25), describe your situation, and ask for the literature that will give you advice on getting started. Ask also for the latest catalogue of the Preservation Bookshop, the National Trust store that sells books having to do with historic preservation. Ask to receive the newsletter put out by the Trust's Legal Services Department, which will keep you up to date on preservation law.

Join Preservation Action, a registered national lobby whose purpose is to influence Congress in favor of historic preservation. For information, write Preservation Action, 2101 L Street, N.W., Suite 906, Washington, D.C. 20037.

Write to the Advisory Council on Historic Preservation, Suite 430, 1522 K Street, N.W., Washington, D.C. 20005. This is the president's official advisory board on federal actions that affect historic preservation. It advises on federal projects and also reports on federal legislation. Its reports are very useful in keeping up with the state of federal law.

Subscribe to *American Preservation,* Bracy House, 620 E. 6th Street, Little Rock, Arkansas 72202. This is a new magazine, appearing six times a year. Subscription, $12. Well-written, well-illustrated stories of projects around the country along with the latest news.

Subscribe to *Small Town,* a monthly magazine published by the Small Towns Institute, P.O. Box 517, Ellensburg, Washington 98926. Personal membership in the Institute (including subscription), $15; institutional membership, $25. The magazine discusses small-town life in many aspects, though it is not specifically interested in historic preservation. However, Volume 8, number 8 (March 1975) was on "historic preservation in small communities," and should be consulted if it is convenient.

Make contact with your state historic preservation officer, your state's official who is in contact with the U.S. Department of the Interior. He has a number of responsibilities: to supervise historic-preservation surveys and planning; to nominate National Register properties; to consult with groups like yours; to administer U.S. Department of the Interior Grants; and to screen cases of National Register properties that may be affected by federal or federally sponsored projects before the Advisory Council on Historic Preservation investigates them. The historic preservation officer is a very important person to know. See Appendix 2 for addresses.

For information on foundations that may support historic preservation projects, write: The Foundation Center, 888 Seventh Avenue, New York, N.Y. 10019.

Look through the following bibliography for books and articles that may be useful.

Appendix 2:
State Historic Preservation Officers

Alabama
Director, Alabama Department of
  Archives and History, Chairman,
Alabama Historical Commission
Archives and History Building
Montgomery, AL 36104

Alaska
Chief of History and Archeology
Division of Parks
Department of Natural Resources
619 Warehouse Avenue, Suite
  210
Anchorage, AK 99501

American Samoa
Territorial Historic Preservation
  Officer
Department of Public Works
Government of American Samoa
Pago Pago, American Samoa
  96799

Arizona
Chief, Natural and Cultural
  Resource
Conservation Section
Arizona State Parks
1688 West Adams
Phoenix, AZ 85007

Arkansas
Director, Arkansas Historic
  Preservation Program
Suite 500, Continental Building
Markham & Main Streets
Little Rock, AR 72201

California
Office of Historic Preservation
Department of Parks & Recreation
P.O. Box 2390
Sacramento, CA 95811

Colorado
Chairman, State Historical Society
Colorado State Museum
200 14th Avenue
Denver, CO 80203

Connecticut
Director, Connecticut Historical
  Commission
59 South Prospect Street
Hartford, CT 06106

Delaware
Director, Division of Historical
  & Cultural Affairs
Hall of Records
Dover, DE 19901

District of Columbia
Director, Department of Housing
    & Community Development
1325 G Street, NW
Washington, D.C. 20005

Florida
Director, Division of Archives,
    History & Records Management
Department of State
401 East Gaines Street
Tallahassee, FL 32304

Georgia
Chief, Historic Preservation
    Section
Department of Natural Resources
270 Washington St., SW, Rm
703-C
Atlanta, GA 30334

Guam
Director of Parks & Recreation
Government of Guam
P.O. Box 682
Agana, Guam 96910

Hawaii
Dept. of Land & Natural
    Resources
P.O. Box 621
Honolulu, HI 96809

Idaho
Historic Preservation Coordinator
Idaho Historical Society
610 North Julia Davis Drive
Boise, ID 83706

Illinois
Director, Dept. of Conservation
602 State Office Building
400 South Spring Street
Springfield, IL 62706

Indiana
Director, Dept. of Natural
    Resources
608 State Office Building
Indianapolis, IN 46204

Iowa
Director, Iowa State Historical
    Department
Division of Historic Preservation
26 East Market Street
Iowa City, IA 52240

Kansas
Executive Director
Kansas State Historical Society
120 West 10th Street
Topeka, KS 66612

Kentucky
Director, Kentucky Heritage
    Comm.
104 Bridge Street
Frankfort, KY 40601

Louisiana
Secretary, Dept. of Culture,
    Recreation, and Tourism
P.O. Box 44361
Baton Rouge, LA 70804

Maine
Director, Maine Historic
   Preservation Commission
31 Western Avenue
Augusta, ME 04330

Maryland
John Shaw House
21 State Circle
Annapolis, MD 21401

Massachusetts
Executive Director, Massachusetts
   Historical Commission
294 Washington Street
Boston, MA 02108

Michigan
Director, Michigan History
   Division
Department of State
Lansing, MI 48918

Minnesota
Director, Minn. Historical Society
690 Cedar Street
St. Paul, MN 55101

Mississippi
Director, State of Mississippi
   Dept. of Archives & History
P.O. Box 571
Jackson, MS 39205

Missouri
Director, State Dept.
   of Natural Resources
1014 Madison Street
Jefferson City, MO 65101

Montana
Director, Montana Historical
   Society
225 North Roberts Street
Veterans' Memorial Building
Helena, MT 59601

Nebraska
Director, The Nebraska State
   Historical Society
1500 R Street
Lincoln, NB 68508

Nevada
Division of Historic Preservation
   & Archeology
Department of Conservation
   & Natural Resources
Nye Building
201 South Fall Street
Carson City, NV 89710

New Hampshire
Commissioner, Dept. of
   Resources and Economic
   Development
P.O. Box 846
Concord, NH 03301

New Jersey
Commissioner, Department of
   Environmental Protection
P.O. Box 1420
Trenton, NJ 08625

New Mexico
State Planning Office
505 Don Gaspar
Santa Fe, NM 87503

New York
Commissioner, Parks &
  Recreation
Agency Building #1
Empire State Plaza
Albany, NY 12238

North Carolina
Director, Div. of Archives &
  History
Department of Cultural Resources
109 East Jones Street
Raleigh, NC 27611

North Dakota
Supt., State Historical Society
Liberty Memorial Building
Bismarck, ND 58501

Oklahoma
State Historic Preservation Officer
235 Pasteur Building
1111 North Lee
Oklahoma City, OK 73103

Oregon
State Parks Superintendent
525 Trade Street, SE
Salem, OR 97310

Pennsylvania
State Historic Preservation
  Officer, Pennsylvania Historical &
  Museum Commission
P.O. Box 1026
Harrisburg, PA 17120

**Commonwealth of Puerto
Rico**
Institute of Puerto Rico Culture
Apartado 4184
San Juan, Puerto Rico 00905

Rhode Island
Director, Department of
  Community Affairs
150 Washington Street
Providence, RI 02903

South Carolina
Director, State Archives
  Department
1430 Senate Street
Columbia, SC 29211

South Dakota
Historical Preservation Center
University of South Dakota
Alumni House
Vermillion, SD 57069

Tennessee
Executive Director, Tennessee
  Historical Commission
170 Second Avenue North, Suite
  100
Nashville, TN 37219

Texas
Executive Director, Texas State
  Historical Commission
P.O. Box 12276
Capitol Station
Austin, TX 78711

**Trust Territory of the
Pacific Islands**
Land Resources Branch
Dept. of Resources &
  Development
Trust Territory of the Pacific
  Islands
Saipan, Mariana Islands 96950

Utah
Executive Director, Department of
   Development Services
Room 104, State Capitol
Salt Lake City, UT 84114

Vermont
Director, Vermont Div. for
   Historic Preservation
Pavilion Office Building
Montpelier, VT 05602

Virginia
Virginia Historic Landmarks
   Comm.
221 Governor Street
Richmond, VA 23219

Virgin Islands
Planning Director, Virgin Islands
   Planning Board
Charlotte Amalie, St. Thomas
Virgin Islands 00801

Washington
State Office of Archeology
   & Historic Preservation
7150 Cleanwater Lane
Olympia, WA 98504

West Virginia
Historic Preservation Unit
Department of Culture & History
State Capitol Complex
Charleston, WV 25305

Wisconsin
Director, State Historical Society
816 State Street
Madison, WI 53706

Wyoming
Director, Recreation Commission
604 East 25th Street, Box 309
Cheyenne, WY 82001

Bibliography

This list of books and articles is subdivided as the text of this book is. We are not advising you to read everything; that would be out of the question; but we are saying that reading some of these books may be useful. The historic preservation situation keeps changing, especially in the area of law, so take care to keep up with things.

General Reading

A Bibliography for Neighborhood Leaders. Washington, D.C.: National Trust for Historic Preservation, n.d.
> A 23-page list of books and helpful hints for leaders of neighborhood organizations.

Bullock, Helen Duprey. Seven Basic Steps for Preserving Historic Sites and Buildings. Washington, D.C.: National Trust for Historic Preservation, n.d.

Federal Programs for Neighborhood Conservation. Washington, D.C.: Advisory Council on Historic Preservation, 1522 K Street, N.W., n.d.

Federal Register. Washington. D.C.: U.S. Government Printing Office, n.d.
> Documents regulations, procedures, etc., of all U.S. government agencies. $50 a year.

Finley, David E. History of the National Trust for Historic Preservation. Washington, D.C.: National Trust, 1965

Guide to Federal Program for Rural Development. Washington, D.C.: Rural Development Service, U.S. Dept. of Agriculture, n.d.

Guide to State Historic Preservation Programs. Washington, D.C.: Preservation Press, National Trust, 1976.
> Guide covers the 50 states, the District of Columbia, and territories, outlining state historic preservation and related legislation, state preservation office procedures for implementing the National Historic Preservation Act of 1966, and state preservation programs. Preservation legislation is categorized into archaeology, archives and historical commissions, historic districts, historic preservation, and state parks and historic sites. Preservation-related legislation categories include civil liability, crimes, environmental quality, historic trails, open space, outdoor recreation, taxation, and tort liability. Special information on easements is included with each entry.

Hosmer, Charles Bridgham. Presence of the Past: A History of the Preservation Movement in the United States before Williamsburg. New York: Putnam, 1965.
> How the movement developed before 1927.

National Trust for Historic Preservation. *A Guide to Federal Programs*. Washington: National Trust, 1974.

Comprehensive reference book on federal preservation-related programs, services, and activities of 49 permanent departments, agencies, boards, and commissions as of June 30, 1974. Compiled by the National Trust with the advice and assistance of the Advisory Council and the Legislative Research Service of the Library of Congress. Each of the 229 entries is catalogued according to the agency and subsidiary office responsible for the activity being described. The program itself is further classified into one or more categories of topics useful to preservationists. Provides the title and a description of each project, an example of its implementation, and the address of a central office to contact for further information.Information needs to be supplemented with new information. There is a 1976 supplement to the *Guide.*

Neighborhood Preservation: A Catalog of Local Programs. Washington, D.C.: Superintendent of Documents, U.S. Government Printing Office, n.d.

Whyte, William H. *The Last Landscape.* Garden City, N.Y.: Doubleday, 1968. Strategies for defending open space.

The Nature of Your Intentions

Historic Preservation Tomorrow. Williamsburg: National Trust for Historic Preservation and Colonial Williamsburg, 1967. Revised edition of principles and guidelines for historic preservation in the United States. Second workshop, Williamsburg, Virginia.

Forming an Organization

Burns, William A. "Trustees: Duties and Responsibilities." *Museum News,* December 1962, pp. 22–23.

Hassard, Howard. "Legal Responsibilities of Historic Society Trustees." *History News,* February 1962, pp. 57–59.

Raymond, Parish, Pine & Plavnick. *Establishing an Historic District: A Guideline for Historic Preservation.* Annapolis, Maryland: Maryland Historic Trust and Department of Economic & Community Development, 1973.

Includes a description of the duties and membership of a historic district commission.

Smith, Michael J. *Heritage Projects: A Practical Guide for Community Preservation Organizations.* Michigan Department of State, 1975.

Wieal, Michael F., III. "Historic District Ordinances: Landmarks Commission Ordinances." Mimeographed. National Trust (1973).

Discusses various ordinances, distinctions between historic district commissions and landmarks commissions, and historic district ordinance litigation. Cites representative cases and lists publications on legal aspects of historic preservation.

Surveys

Brown, Theodore M. "The Importance and Use of Surveys." *Historic Preservation,* October 1963.

Derry, Ann, and others. *Guidelines for Local Surveys: A Basis for Preservation Planning.* Washington, D.C.: National Register of Historic Places, U.S. Department of the Interior, 1977.

    An official guide to survey-making with abundant material on every aspect of this important preservation technique; discusses publications, as well.

McKee, Harley J. *Recording Historic Buildings.* Washington, D.C.: U.S. Government Printing Office, 1970.

    A statement of the principles and standards for recording architecture, used by the Historic American Buildings Survey, U.S. Department of the Interior. A compilation of material reflecting HABS practices and including a discussion of the HABS Inventory, landscape architecture, area studies, historic districts, history of planning, civil engineering, and industrial archaeology. Bibliography provided.

Massachusetts Historical Commission. *Guide to Inventory Techniques.* Boston: Massachusetts Historical Commission, 1970.

Massey, James C. *The Architectural Survey.* Washington, D.C.: National Trust, 1969.

Morton, Terry Brust. "The Published Architectural Survey." *Historic Preservation,* 1964.

New York State Board for Historic Preservation. *Historic Resources Survey Manual,* 1972.

The National Registers

Conserving America's Neighborhoods: Selections from the National Register. Washington, D.C.: Department of the Interior, 1976.

    Limited copies of preliminary work available from the National Register. An expanded work is in progress.

11593. Washington, D.C.: Department of the Interior.

    This bi-monthly technical bulletin is produced within the National Register Division and is available at major universities and libraries across the country. A limited number of copies are available from the National Register Division, Office of Archaeology and Historic Preservation.

How to Complete National Register Forms. Washington, D.C.: National Register Division, 1977. GPO Stock No. 024-005-00666-4. Price, $1.35.

The National Register.

    A significant function of the National Register is publishing the list of registered properties. The latest hard-cover volume containing some 10,000 entries was published in 1976, and a supplement to that work is in progress. A cumulative listing of all N.R. properties is published each February in the *Federal Register,* and additions to the list are printed usually on the first Tuesday of each month. These *Federal Register* listings and the 1976 hard-cover volumes are available from the Superintendent of Documents, U.S. Government Printing Office, Washington, D.C. 20402.

The National Register of Historic Places. Washington, D.C.: National Register Division, 1976. GPO Stock No. 024-005-00645-1. Price, $13.

National Register of Historic Places.

Information leaflet available from the National Register upon request.

Publications and Publicity

Wrenn, Tony P. "The Tourist Industry and Promotional Publications." *Historic Preservation,* July 1964.

Legal Devices

Advisory Council on Historic Preservation. *Digest of Cases, 1967–1973.* Washington, D.C.: U.S. Government Printing Office, 1973.

Cases considered under Section 106 of the National Historic Preservation Act of 1966 and Section 2 (b) of Executive Order 11593, Protection and Enhancement of the Cultural Environment (May 13, 1971). Under these sections, the Advisory Council is charged with reviewing the effect of federal projects and actions on properties on, or eligible for, the National Register of Historic Places. Although the majority of historic preservation cases have been settled by negotiation as prescribed by Advisory Council procedures published in 38 *Federal Register* 5388 (1973), 26 cases have required council consideration and formal hearings. The synopses of these cases provide information on compliance, the council approach to adverse activities and suggestions for minimizing effects on historic areas.

Allen, Paul. *Conservation Easements.* Baltimore: Maryland Environmental Trust, 1974.

Booklet discussing the use of the conservation easement to preserve land or buildings. While the emphasis is on Maryland law, there are useful guidelines of general application to all situations. There is an overview of the easement, its legal foundation and potential use, and an outline of the probable tax consequences of an easement donation.

Biddle, James. "Federal Legislation and Historic Preservation." *Museum News,* April 1968.

A brief descriptive analysis and evaluation of the National Historic Preservation Act of 1966. Includes complete text of the law.

Brenneman, Russell L. *Should Easements Be Used to Protect National Historic Landmarks?* Washington, D.C.: U.S. Department of the Interior, 1975.

Vol. 1: Use of easements for historic preservation.

Vol. 2: Bibliography, statutes, Internal Revenue Service code.

Vol. 3: Copies of easement instruments and covenants.

Codeman, John. "A Law for the Preservation of a Historic District." *Historic Preservation,* April 1962.

A short article on things to consider in drafting a historic preservation law.

Council on Environmental Quality. *Environmental Quality. The Second Annual Report.* Washington, D.C.: U.S. Government Printing Office, 1971.

The National Environment Policy Act of 1969 required an annual report of the Council on Environmental Quality. Included is a section on preserving historic buildings that presents a summary of current laws assisting building preservation. The appendix provides the text of Executive Order 11593, Protection and Enhancement of the Cultural Environment (May 13, 1971).

Council on Environmental Quality. *The Taking Issue: An Analysis of the Constitutional Limits of Land Use Control.* Washington, D.C.: U.S. Government Printing Office, 1973.

"Federal Responsibility in Historic Preservation," *Historic Preservation,* January 1968.

Edited proceedings of a meeting held to inform the public about federal preservation programs in the U.S. Departments of the Interior, Transportation, and Housing and Urban Development, followed by case studies of particular applications of these programs in local areas.

Gray, Oscar S. *Cases and Materials on Environmental Law.* Washington, D.C.: Bureau of National Affairs, 1970.

Guidelines for State Historic Preservation Legislation. Washington, D.C.: Advisory Council on Historic Preservation, 1972.

Guidelines prepared at the National Symposium on State Environmental Legislation, Historic Preservation Workshop, held March 15–18, 1972. The guidelines propose a comprehensive legislative program for state and local government involvement in preservation. It is suggested that the fundamental responsibility for preservation activities be assigned to a state historic preservation agency with a state advisory council co-ordinating government activities that affect historic properties and a state historical trust generating activities in the private sector. The guidelines also include proposed local enabling provisions to stimulate comprehensive preservation programs and suggestions for legislation protecting from development archaeological resources and underwater properties. Suggestions for tax incentives for private preservation activities are presented.

"Historic District Ordinances: Landmarks Commission Ordinances." Mimeographed. Washington, D.C.: National Trust for Historic Preservation, 1973.

The Law in Preservation Issues. Washington, D.C.: National Trust for Historic Preservation, 1971.

Legal Techniques in Historic Preservation. Washington, D.C.: National Trust for Historic Preservation, 1971.

Articles on historic preservation law from papers presented at the conference on Legal Techniques in Preservation sponsored by the Trust in May 1971, in Washington. Generally, the papers in this volume deal with the policy and operational implications of federal legislation related to historic preservation. All articles are annotated individually in this bibliography. This publication supplements the historic preservation issue of *Law and Contemporary Problems.*

Montague, Robert L., and Tony P. Wrenn. *Planning for Preservation.* Chicago: American Society of Planning Officials, 1964.

A summary of legal problems, trends, and legislative safeguards in historic preservation. Includes discussions of economic effects of preservation—specifically, increased property values and profits from the tourist trade.

Morrison, Jacob H. *Historic Preservation Law,* 2d ed. Washington, D.C.: National Trust for Historic Preservation, 1974.

Morrison, Jacob H. *Supplement to Historic Preservation Law.* New Orleans: Jacob H. Morrison, 1972.

Update of the 1965 edition of the Morrison volume on historic preservation law. Morrison discusses principal federal legislation; state and local statutes and ordinances covering such areas as tax exemption, eminent domain, and historic district; and court decisions on aesthetic zoning, highway beautification, and historic preservation. Appendix contains state statutes. Invaluable source and general aid for preservation attorneys. Contact: Preservation Bookshop, National Trust.

Nelson, Gaylord. "Scenic Easements and Preservation." *Historic Preservation,* July 1965.

Preservation in Your Town: The Legal Framework. Mimeographed. Washington, D.C.: National Trust for Historic Preservation, 1973.

Text of address delivered at the 27th annual meeting of the National Trust. Outlines characteristic of local historic preservation ordinances and contrasts historic district ordinances with landmarks ordinances. Brief mention of facade easements as a companion legal technique to zoning.

Recent Historic Preservation Law Developments. Mimeographed. Washington, D.C.: National Trust for Historic Preservation, 1974.

Fact sheet summarizing four significant 1974 court decisions that uphold various historic-preservation activities. Two cases consider the constitutionality of barring the demolition of historic buildings. The third deals with the suspension of issuance of building permits in a proposed historic district pending an architectural survey. The fourth case distinguishes historic-district zoning from conventional zoning.

Stipe, Robert E. "Easement *vs.* Zoning: Preservation Tools." *Historic Preservation,* April 1968.

Summary of the Housing and Community Development Act of 1974. Washington, D.C.: U.S. Department of Housing and Urban Development, 1974.

Outline of the 1974 omnibus legislation that significantly alters federal involvement in local housing and community development activities. Of special importance to preservationists is Title I of the act, which creates a single program of Community Development block grants. Describes, among other things, purposes of Title I; what a community must do to secure funding; permissible use of funds; and the scope of federal review. Outlines the major features of revised Section 701 comprehensive planning grants, which includes grants to develop and implement plans to survey sites and structures of historical and architectural value.

Wiedl, Michael F., III. *Historic Building Criteria for Historic Districts and Individual Landmarks.* Mimeographed. Washington, D.C.: National Trust for Historic Preservation, 1973.

    A guide to historic-district ordinances and statutes, landmark ordinances, and nonstatutory historic building criteria. Cites standards used in evaluating an application to demolish or alter the exterior of a historic building.

Wiedl, Michael F., III. *Preservation in Your Town: The Legal Framework.* Mimeographed. Washington, D.C.: National Trust for Historic Preservation, 1973.

Wrenn, Tony P. *Preservation Legislation.* Washington, D.C.: National Trust for Historic Preservation, 1965.

Master Planning

Montague, Robert, and Tony P. Wrenn. *Planning for Preservation,* Chicago: American Society of Planning Officials, 1964.

Finance

Catalog of Federal Domestic Assistance. Washington, D.C.: U.S. Government Printing Office, yearly.

    Lists all federal programs of use in housing rehabilitation, whether offering goods or services. Price, $20 annually.

Information: Factors Affecting Valuation of Historic Property. Washington, D.C.: National Trust for Historic Preservation, 1976.

    A nine-page guide to the subject.

Murtagh, William J. "Financing Landmark Preservation." *AIA Journal,* March 1966. Reprint for the National Trust for Historic Preservation.

Preservation and the Tax Reform Act of 1976. Washington, D.C.: *Preservation News* (National Trust for Historic Preservation), 1977.

    Explains the meaning of the Tax Reform Act for preservationists and gives typical examples of its application. Should be supplemented with later information on "technical amendments" and interpretations by the IRS.

Sheehan, Donald T. "Programming for Fund-raising." *Historic Preservation,* 1966.

Sources of Funding for Historic Preservation, Guide No. 4. Annapolis, Md.: Maryland Historical Trust, n.d.

    Booklet describing methods of obtaining funds for historic preservation activities. Includes outlines of major federal, Maryland state and private sources of funds, such as the National Trust, America the Beautiful Fund, and numerous foundations. Brief discussion of methods of funding at the local level: setting up a revolving fund; mortgaging properties; buying, restoring, and selling property; property exchange. Easements, development rights transfer, and tax-exempt bonds are mentioned as means of reducing that cost of restoration.

Ziegler, Arthur P., Jr., Leopold Adler II, and Walter C. Kidney. *Revolving Funds for Historic Preservation*. Pittsburgh: Ober Park Associates, 1975.
> For information, write Ober Park Associates, Allegheny Square West, Pittsburgh, Pennsylvania 15212.

Preserving a Property

Architectural Record. December 1977.
> Special issue devoted to "New Life for Old Buildings."

Bowsher, Alice Meriwether. *Design Review in Historic Districts: A handbook for Virginia Review Boards*. Inquire of Alice M. Bowsher, 5 Norman Drive, Birmingham, Ala. 35213.
> A general guide to those attempting to control new construction and remodeling in historic districts. Applied specifically to Virginia conditions, but much of the material is applicable everywhere.

Brightman, Anna. *Window Treatment for Historic Houses, 1700–1850*. Washington, D.C.: National Trust for Historic Preservation, 1967.

Bullock, Orin M., Jr. *The Restoration Manual: An Illustrated Guide to the Preservation and Restoration of Old Buildings*. Norwalk, Connecticut, 1966.

Gilchrist, Agnes. *A Primer on the Care and Repair of Buildings*. Mount Vernon, N.Y.: Society of Architectural Historians, 1963.

Harrison, Myra F. *Adaptive Use of Historic Structures: A Series of Case Studies*. Washington, D.C.: National Trust for Historic Preservation, 1971.

Ipswich Historical Commission. *Something to Preserve*. Ipswich, Mass.: Ipswich Historical Commission, 1975.
> A very good general account of the preservation campaign in Ipswich, with detailed studies of how three houses were preserved and a "common-sense guide to preservation." Much attention, also, to legal matters.

Kidney, Walter C. *Working Places: The Adaptive Use of Industrial Buildings*. Pittsburgh: Ober Park Associates 1974.
> Offers information useful in nonindustrial as well as industrial adaptations. For information, write Ober Park Associates, Allegheny Square West, Pittsburgh, Pa. 15212.

Pitts, Carolyn, and others. *The Cape May Handbook*. Philadelphia: The Athenaeum of Philadelphia, 1977.
> A practical guide to repairs, restoration, and other matters, going into considerable technical detail. Cape May is a town of Victorian frame houses, and the advice given is applicable in most parts of the United States.

Stanforth, Deirdre, and Martha Stamm. *Buying and Renovating a House in the City*. New York, 1972.

Stephen, George. *Remodeling Old Houses Without Destroying Their Character*. New York, 1972.

Ziegler, Arthur P., Jr. *Historic Preservation in Inner-City Areas: A Manual of Practice*. Pittsburgh: Ober Park Associates, 1971.

Supplementary Bibliography

Reprinted by permission from *Rural Conservation,* an Information Sheet published by the National Trust for Historic Preservation. Copyright © 1979 by The Preservation Press, National Trust for Historic Preservation in the United States.

Allagash Environmental Institute. *The Comparative Economics of Residential Development and Open Space Conservation, A Manual for Municipal Officials and Other Townspeople.* Portland, Maine: Author, 1977. 118 pp., $3.50. (Available from Maine Coast Heritage Trust, 60 Main Street, Bar Harbor, Maine 04609).

Provides a method for determining what the general economic impact of a proposed residential development or open space plan will be on municipal expenditures over a period of time; includes work sheets and explanations of economic formulas.

American Law Institute. *A Model Land Development Code.* Washington, D.C.: Author, 1976.

Model code and commentary on land-use control; provides much information on techniques that can be used for rural preservation, such as preservation districts, planned unit developments and land banks.

Brenneman, Russell L. *Private Approaches to the Preservation of Open Land.* New London, Conn.: The Conservation and Research Foundation, 1967. 133 pp., $8 hardbound; $6 softbound. (Box 1445, Connecticut College, New London, Conn. 06320).

Analyzes legal approaches available to private citizens for preserving open land; discusses fee simple, trust, leasehold and restrictive covenant techniques; summarizes tax aspects of preserving open land; lists public programs and sample documents.

————. "Should Easements Be Used to Protect National Historic Landmarks?"—A Study for the National Park Service. 1975. 3 volumes. (Available at special libraries).

An unpublished study; comprehensive description of past use of easements for protecting historic properties and landmarks, volume I; bibliogra-

134

phy, federal documents and state statutes, volume II; sample easement instruments, volume III.

Browne, Kingsbury, ed. *Case Studies in Land Conservation.* Boston: New England Natural Resources Center, 1977. $5.00 (3 Joy Street, Boston, Mass. 02108).

Examples of land conservation projects; editorial notes explain specific conservation tools. The six case studies cover local conservation organizations and land trusts, federal programs, The Nature Conservancy, conservation easements and lobbying of conservation organizations.

Council on Environmental Quality. *Environmental Quality.* Washington, D.C.: U.S. Government Printing Office, annual, price varies.

Reports on environmental developments during the year; includes an update on legislation; 1978 edition contains the new NEPA regulations, essays on agricultural land and the protection of special areas, including coastal zones, greenline parks, floodplains and wetlands.

Davidson, Joan and Wibberley, Gerald. *Planning and the Rural Environment.* Oxford and New York: Pergamon Press, 1977. 227 pp., $17 hardbound; $9.50 softbound.

Explores the complexity of issues in planning the English countryside; historical development of countryside planning, diversity of rural interest groups; problems and concerns in resource planning, agriculture, forestry, recreational areas, wildlife and landscape conservation.

French and Pickering Creeks Conservation Trust. *Preaching of the Conference on Voluntary Preservation of Open Space.* Pottstown, Pa.: Author, 1974. 102 pp., $5.00. (Box 360, R.D. 2, Pottstown, Pa. 19464).

Examines the legal and tax aspects of conservation easements; describes their use by environmental organizations.

Guitar, Mary Anne. *Property Power: How to Keep the Bulldozer, the Power Line and the Highwaymen from Your Door.* Garden City, N.Y.: Doubleday & Company, Inc., 1972. 322 pp., $6.95.

Presents the political and environmental issues involved in land-use planning; case studies show how citizens can influence local planning decisions; discusses such techniques as easements, land trusts and incentive policies.

Healy, Robert G. *Land Use and the States.* Washington, D.C.: Resources for the Future, Inc., 1976. 233 pp., $2.95. (1755 Massachusetts Avenue, N.W., Washington, D.C. 20036).

Examines the states' role in land-use planning; analyzes current state programs; concludes with general proposals for better coordination of state controls; case studies of Vermont's Act 250, California's Coastal Zone Conservation Act and Florida's Environmental Land and Water Management Act.

Hendler, Bruce. *Caring for the Land, Environmental Principles for Site Design and Review.* Chicago, Ill.: American Society of Planning Officials, 1977. 94 pp., $9.00.

Discussion of the principles and techniques for good site planning and design of new construction and subdivision including considerations for visual impact.

Housing Assistance Council. *A Guide to Housing and Community Development Programs for Small Towns and Rural Areas.* Washington, D.C.: Author, 1977. 81 pp., $6.00 (1828 L Street, N.W., Washington, D.C. 20036).

Descriptions of federal housing and community development programs for small towns and rural areas; lists agency contacts.

King, Thomas F. *The Archeological Survey: Methods and Uses.* Washington, D.C.: Heritage Conservation and Recreation Service, U.S. Department of the Interior, 1978. 134 pp., $3.25. Available from U.S. Government Printing Office, Washington, D.C. 20402. GPO Stock No. 024-016-00091-9.

Lassey, William R. *Planning in Rural Environments.* New York: McGraw-Hill, Inc., 1977. 257 pp., $14.95.

Study of rural planning in the United States; explains basic concepts, results of research, planning procedures and management tools for effective rural planning; describes the rural planning process in the Netherlands and the United Kingdom.

McHarg, Ian L. *Design With Nature.* Garden City, N.Y.: Doubleday & Company, Inc., 1971. 198 pp., $6.95.

Essays and case studies stressing the need for environmental design that relate to the natural conditions of an area; environment used as a determinant in the planning process.

Marshall, James H. M., and White, W. P. Dinsmoor. *Environmental Conservation: A Citizens' Sourcebook.* Warrenton, Va.: Piedmont Environmental Council, 1975. 199 pp., $4.95. (28-C Main Street, Warrenton, Va. 22186).

Case studies from northern Virginia presenting planning, visual environment and conservation issues; examples of how local organizations deal with rural conservation concerns.

Maryland Environmental Trust. *Conservation Easements.* Baltimore: Author, 1974. 24 pp., free. (8 East Mulberry Street, Baltimore, Md. 21202).

Explanation of one state's conservation easement program.

National Register of Historic Places. *Guidelines for Local Surveys: A Basis for Preservation Planning.* Washington, D.C.: U.S. Department of the Interior, 1977. 83 pp., $2.50. Available from the U.S. Government Printing Office, Washington, D.C. 20402. GPO Stock No. 024-016-00089-7.

A how-to publication on planning and conducting a historic resources survey; emphasis on using survey data for planning.

————. National Register informational brochure. Washington, D.C.: U.S. Department of the Interior, 1978. 13 pp., free.

Basic information on the National Register of Historic Places program; lists addresses of the state historic preservation officers.

National Rural Center. *A Directory of Rural Organizations.* Washington, D.C.: Author, 1977. 53 pp. First copy free, extra copies $2.00 each.

Listing of national organizations and agencies involved in rural development and revitalization.

————. *Private Funding for Rural Programs.* Washington, D.C.: Author, 1978. 63 pp. First copy free, extra copies $2.00 each.

Directory of more than 50 national, regional and local foundations that fund rural projects and programs.

————. *Resource Guide for Rural Development.* Washington, D.C.: Author, 1978. 150 pp. First copy free, extra copies $5.00 each.

Listing of various assistance programs for rural development.

National Trust for Historic Preservation. "Basic Preservation Procedures." National Trust Information sheet.** (To be published in 1979.)

————. *Preservation News.* * Monthly newspaper reporting on national events in historic preservation.

————. *Public Funds for Historic Preservation.* Nancy Shirk. 1977. National Trust Information sheet.**

————. *Working with Local Government.* Leila Smith. 1977. National Trust Information sheet.**

National Wildlife Federation. *Conservation Directory.* Washington, D.C.: Author, annual, 1979 edition. 271 pp., $4.00. (1412 16th Street, N.W., Washington, D.C. 20036).

Lists private organizations and government agencies at the national, state and local levels concerned with all aspects of conservation; contains a short description of each organization and agency, names and key officials, addresses and telephone numbers.

Natural Resources Defense Council, Inc. *Land Use Controls in the United States: A Handbook on the Legal Rights of Citizens.* New York: The Dial Press, 1977. 362 pp., $7.95.

Describes legal techniques at various levels of government for controlling or influencing the use of land; discusses means for citizen involvement.

Northeast Environmental Design. *The Vermont Backroad—A Guide for the Protection, Conservation, and Enhancement of Its Scenic Quality.* Woodstock, Vermont: Author, 1974. 69 pp., $4.00. (Ottauquechee Regional Planning and Development Commission, 39 Central Street, Woodstock, Vt. 05091).

Provides guidelines for design, construction and maintenance of scenic roads.

Reilly, William K., ed. *The Use of Land: A Citizen's Policy Guide to Urban Growth.* New York: Thomas Y. Crowell Co., 1973. 318 pp., $3.95.

Describes attitudes toward land use and urban growth; surveys national and state land-use legislation; determines desirable long-term planning trends and recommends approaches for historic preservation, open space protection and zoning policies; includes essay on subdivision of rural land.

River Conservation Fund. *Flowing Free, A Citizen's Guide for Protecting Wild and Scenic Rivers.* Washington, D.C.: Author, 1977. 76 pp., $3.25. (317 Pennsylvania Avenue, S.E., Washington, D.C. 20003).

Information on designating and protecting wild and scenic rivers; explains the federal wild and scenic rivers program, state protection programs and local protection techniques; presents guidelines for citizen activities and includes three case studies.

Rural America. *ruralamerica, A Voice for Small Town and Rural People.* Monthly newsjournal. Washington, D.C.: Author. Subscription $15 a year. (1346 Connecticut Avenue, N.W., Washington, D.C. 20036).

Covers a wide range of rural issues.

Shopsin, William C. *Saving Large Estates: Conservation, Historic Preservation, Adaptive Re-Use.* Setauket, N.Y.: Society for the Preservation of Long Island Antiquities and the New York State Council on the Arts, 1977. 199 pp., $8.00. (SPLIA, 93 North Country Road, Setauket, N.Y. 11733).

Essays and case studies concentrating on the preservation of country estates; studies various planning and conservation approaches, tax policies and adaptive use possibilities; investigates efforts in New York's Long Island, Westchester and Dutchess counties and the Adirondack-Catskill regions.

Small Town Institute. *Small Town*. Monthly magazine. Ellensburg, Wash.: Author. Subscription $15 a year. (P.O. Box 517, Ellensburg, Wash. 98926).

Dedicated to the study of issues and resources involving American small towns and the countryside; source of information on new programs and publications.

Stone, Edward H. *Visual Resource Management*. Washington, D.C.: American Society of Landscape Architects, 1978. 32 pp., $5.00. (ASLA, 1900 M Street, N.W., Suite 750, Washington, D.C. 20036).

Describes elements of visual analysis and methods of land management to retain significant visual resources; annotated list of publications and studies about this process.

Toner, William. *Saving Farms and Farmland: A Community Guide*. Chicago: American Society of Planning Officials, 1978. 45 pp., $6.00. (American Planning Association, 1313 East 60th Street, Chicago, ILL. 60637).

Examines the issues of farmland retention in the United States; analyzes techniques and programs.

U.S. Department of Agriculture, Committee on Land Use. *Land Use Notes*. Washington, D.C.: U.S. Department of Agriculture. (Soil Conservation Service, Warren T. Zitzmann, ed.) Free.

Newsletter devoted to land-use issues.

————. Economic Research Service. *Rural Zoning in the United States: Analysis of Enabling Legislation*. Washington, D.C.: U.S. Department of Agriculture, 1972. 170 pp., $1.50. Available from U.S. Government Printing Office, Washington, D.C. 20402. GPO Stock No. 0100-2519.

Discussion of rural zoning issues; surveys regional, state and local approaches; presents basic elements and procedures of a rural zoning ordinance; cites innovations and trends in recent zoning enabling legislation; discusses use of zoning powers to protect rural resources.

————. Soil Conservation Service. *Procedure to Establish Priorities in Landscape Architecture*. Washington, D.C.: Author, 1978. 19 pp., free.

Describes procedures for evaluating resources and implementing data into the planning and design of projects.

Virginia Outdoors Foundation. *Virginia Outdoors Foundation*. Informational Brochure. Richmond: Author, 1976. Free. (803 East Broad Street, Richmond, Va. 23219).

Explanation of one state's conservation easement program.

Whyte, William H. *The Last Landscape.* Garden City, N.Y.: Doubleday & Co., Inc., 1968. 428 pp., $7.95 hardbound; $2.95 softbound.

Primer on the issues, techniques and planning alternatives in open space, landscape and environmental protection; cites specific programs and case studies.

Wrenn, Tony P. *Woodbury, Connecticut: A New England Townscape.* Washington, D.C.: Preservation Press, National Trust for Historic Preservation, 1975. 60 pp., $3.00.*

Case study of a rural Connecticut community; describes the community's townscape and heritage; identifies the need to preserve surrounding landscape that enhances the town's setting; proposes several courses of action through a cultural rural landscape program.

Zube, Ervin H., Brush, Robert O., and Fabos, Julius Gy, eds. *Landscape Assessment: Value, Perceptions, and Resources.* Stroudsburg, Pa.: Dowden, Hutchinson, Ross, Inc., 1975. 320 pp., $35.

Three-part discussion of the wide range of landscape resources and values and the process of integrating them in environmental planning; covers (1) values associated with the landscape, (2) perception of and response to the visual landscape and (3) development of assessment models for landscape planning and management.

*Available from the National Trust Preservation Bookshop, 1785 Massachusetts Avenue, N.W., Washington, D.C. 20036, at the prices quoted. When ordering publications from the bookshop please add $1.50 to cover postage and handling. Payment must accompany all orders. National Trust members receive a 10 percent discount (before addition of postage and handling).

**Single copies of Information sheets are available through National Trust regional and field offices. Bulk copies at 50 cents each may be ordered from the National Trust Preservation Bookshop at the address above.

Index